THE SPEAKING
OF ENGLISH VERSE

THE SPEAKING
OF ENGLISH VERSE

BY

ELSIE FOGERTY

MCMXXIII
LONDON AND TORONTO
J. M. DENT & SONS LTD.
NEW YORK: E. P. DUTTON & CO.

PRINTED IN GREAT BRITAIN

INTRODUCTION

THE art of poetry owes its great and wonderful power to the fact that it has for its medium man's faculty of speech.

Like all art, poetry seeks to re-create life in terms of its own chosen medium out of delight in that medium.

The painter sees the joy and harmony of life in line and colour. The musician seeks it in sound. The poet in words.

Therefore the word "poetry" calls up to us a double significance, and from the very nature of speech it does this more fully than any of the other arts.

We think of poetry as an attitude to life itself; showing us things which are great, sublime or significant. And so we speak of the "poetry of motion"; of the "poetical attitude to life." Even of a "prose poem." Or again, we speak of poetry in a more definite and formal sense when we mean the expression of these things in ordered and harmonious patterns of words: in what we call verse. Here we feel something has been created out of words as perfectly as a flower or a jewel, and we cannot divide the harmony of the words from the significance they express. How close this double use of the word "poetry" lies to the very nature of speech may be seen if we consider it a little more deeply. In speech we are conscious first of what is called "content"—of something we wish to say. Then we give this expression by the audible movements of utterance; and in between stands that mysterious and individual

vii

thing which we call vocabulary; this each generation accurately teaches to the next, and the power of speech which results from all these is so intimately our own, so unconsciously ours, that at last we hardly know whether we can or cannot think without words. We only know that it is through words that we limit, order and define our thoughts, till words in turn grow so charged with significance that it is not easy for us to share with others all they convey to us.

The poet is the man who does this most completely, whose mastery of words gives them an appeal so universal that it traverses time, race, class, individuality itself. And it is this "universality" that distinguishes above all other qualities the greatest poetry.

> We are the music-makers,
>   And we are the dreamers of dreams
> Wandering by lone sea-breakers,
>   And sitting by desolate streams;
> World-losers and world-forsakers,
>   On whom the pale moon gleams:
> Yet we are the movers and shakers
>   Of the world for ever, it seems.
>
> With wonderful deathless ditties
> We build up the world's great cities,
>   And out of a fabulous story
>   We fashion an empire's glory:
> One man with a dream, at pleasure,
>   Shall go forth and conquer a crown;
> And three with a new song's measure
>   Can trample an empire down.
>
> We, in the ages lying
>   In the buried past of the earth,
> Built Nineveh with our sighing,
>   And Babel itself with our mirth;

And o'erthrew them with prophesying
To the old of the new world's worth;
For each age is a dream that is dying,
Or one that is coming to birth.

(O'Shaughnessy.)

Is there any way by which we can enter more fully and reverently into the poet's work so that we may give him the one thing he asks of us, understanding of his art?

We recognise perfunctorily the greatness of the poet's gift, yet many people are not at all ashamed—indeed they seem sometimes rather proud—to say "Oh, well, of course, I don't understand poetry and all that sort of thing; it does not appeal to me." Some people are colour-blind; many are tone-deaf; some few are word-blind and cannot trace the meaning of a printed page, but none of these people go about boasting of their deficiencies; they are a little sorrowful, a little ashamed, and one has to cheer them up; often they try every means, however costly, to cure themselves. Some people, in the same way, are rhythm-deaf, and cannot appreciate pattern by the sense of hearing, but the majority of those who do not love poetry are the victims of bad teaching, and we ought to find a way of lifting this burden of deafness from them.

The best way would be a great revival of the art which has declined ever since the multiplication of printed books, the art of speaking verse as the poet wrote and felt it.

Words, unlike harmonies, possess logical meaning, and it is this which blinds us to the fact that many a casual reader knows very little more about a poem by letting his eyes run over and translate the meaning of the words than he would know of the music of a great song by reading the words printed between the musical staves of its score.

If we are to help people to read poetry for themselves, or if we are to venture to act as interpreters, as executive artists, standing between the poet and those who have not the leisure or taste to learn to hear for themselves, we must go through an arduous technical training.

Above all, we must throw away the horrible false tradition of "recitation," which stood self-condemned in that it never succeeded in interpreting anything but the worst, the most vulgar and meaningless of verse, because in that it could find room for the personal self-assertion which destroyed all true faculty of poetic interpretation.

This book is an attempt to set down something of the practical technical knowledge acquired in many years' study of a difficult subject.

It is very slight and very imperfect, but it may serve to help those who will go further, and it may at least prevent a certain number of teachers from involuntarily standing between their students and a love of poetry.

ACKNOWLEDGMENTS

THE author's sincere thanks are due to Dr. W. A. Aikin for permission to reproduce the Diagram of the Resonator Scale and for permission to use some of his privately printed notes, as well as for a general revision of the technical chapters on Speech; to Dr. William Pasteur for reading the proofs of the section on Breathing.

The notes on Position and Movement throughout the book owe much to the work done by Dr. H. Hulbert during the years he was working at the Central School. To Dr. Rouse and Professor Daniel Jones for their kindness in working out the phonetic transcriptions from the Greek and for the interesting experiment in the notation of tonic accent.

To Miss Kathleen Salmon for revision of the musical section and examples.

To Mr. Walter Ripman for the revision of the phonetic notations, though the author is alone responsible for some of the heretical views therein expressed, and also for his kindness in preparing the phonetic transcription of the passage from the *Æneid*, Book IV.

For permission to include certain poems and shorter quotations in prose and verse the author gratefully acknowledges her indebtedness to the following, also acknowledged in the text: John Drinkwater, Siegfried Sassoon, Ralph Hodgson, Hilaire Belloc, John Masefield and Sir Henry Newbolt.

To Professor Granville Bantock for permission to include an example of the setting of the *Electra*.

To Professor W. A. Mackail for permission to include some lines of his prose translations of Sappho from *Lectures on Greek Poetry*.

To the literary executors of James Elroy Flecker, and to Mr. Martin Secker, the publisher of the collected edition of his works.

To the literary executors of Rupert Brooke, and Messrs. Sidgwick and Jackson, publishers of his collected works.

To Messrs. Chatto and Windus for quotations from Robert Louis Stevenson's *Will o' the Mill* and *Romance*.

To Messrs. Longmans Green & Co. for Professor W. A. Mackail's translations.

To the literary executors of Mr. Austin Dobson, and to the Oxford University Press, for the fable from " A Cap that Fits " (*Proverbs in Porcelain*), " Lines on a Fan that belonged to the Marquise de Pompadour," and other quotations.

To the literary executors of Mr. George Macdonald, and Messrs. A. P. Watt and Son, for a triolet from *A Threefold Cord*.

To Mr. John Murray for quotations from Robert Browning and Robert Bridges.

To Messrs. Macmillan, for a quotation from Ralph Hodgson's *Song of Honour*, for a passage from the Preface to William Butler Yeats' *Plays for an Irish Theatre*, for a poem from Mr. James Stephens' *Songs from the Clay*, and for Mr. Andrew Lang's Sonnet, *The Odyssey*.

To Messrs. G. Bell and Sons for lines from Charles Stuart Calverley in their complete edition of his works.

To Mr. Wm. Heinemann for lines from Edmund Gosse's *New Poems*, and from Swinburne's *Poems*.

To Professor Kastner of Manchester University, for permission to use his pointing of lines from *Andromaque*, printed in his *History of French Versification* (Oxford, Clarendon Press).

To the " Libraire Felix Alcan " for an extract from Professor Bergson's work, *Matière et Mémoire*.

To the *Mercure de France* for a sonnet of Albert Samain, originally published in *Poètes d'Aujourd'hui*.

To Messrs. George Allen and Unwin for permission to include certain of my exercises in Speech already published in *First Notes on Speech Training*, and to Miss S. Wellesley-Reade for a similar permission in regard to those published in her *Word Practice* books.

ELSIE FOGERTY,
*Central School of Speech Training and Dramatic Art,
Royal Albert Hall, London.*

NOTE

The following list of symbols used in pointing the marked passages throughout this book will be found useful:

    ˋ To mark a stressed syllable without regard to vowel length.

    ⁻ To mark a long vowel unstressed, or a long unstressed syllable.

    ˘ To mark a short unstressed vowel.

    ° To mark a vowel prolonged by musical tone, particularly in the case of assonance.

    ˘ ˆ To mark a sharp rising or falling inflection, generally antithetic.

In addition to these symbols several passages are marked for duration by a regular musical transcription, see especially Chapter VII., page 170 *et seq.*

The duration marks and tonic accents of the phonetic Greek transcriptions are marked by wave-lengths in measured pitch (page 35 *et seq.*).

The ordinary bar lines used for metric division into feet are used to indicate the grouping of stress rhythms.

Musical notes above and below the printed line are used to indicate lilted stresses in Chapter VI., pages 150 and 151.

A table of the phonetic symbols used will be found in Chapter V., pages 123 and 124, and the numerals of Dr. Aikin's resonator scale in the same chapter, pages 138 and 139, and in the diagram of Appendix II.

It is important to remember that none of these marks must be treated as more than an indication of the effect to be aimed at, and that no rigid regulation of poetic interpretation is either desirable or possible.

Failure to appreciate this leads to the constant

disagreement of different authorities as to the "correct" manner of pointing a passage.

A stress mark, for instance, indicates that a particular syllable is to be given a certain prominence but gives no slightest indication of the *degree* of force required.

A series of stresses equal in metric value may form part of an emotional climax, so that the value of each stress in the series should be greater than the last.

A stress rarely indicates abrupt or clear-cut increase in force. To determine all such questions we must look at the whole character of the verse and of its movement; this is necessary even in the case of the elaborate symbols of musical notation and far more in the speaking of poetry.

In the lines:

> Then I càst loose my buff-coat, each hòlster let fall,
> Shook òff both my jack-boots, let gò belt and all
> (R. BROWNING, *How they brought the*
> *Good News from Ghent to Aix*),

the stresses would be sharp and abrupt, almost like a child's scanning sing-song, as the line suggests the jerking gallop of an exhausted horse.

In such lines as the opening verse of Keats' *Ode to a Nightingale* the stresses point waves of sound and are in no sense percussion marks. Rather successive waves or jets of vocal tone which culminate on each succeeding stress.

These successive pulse-beats of verse are, physiologically, breath-pressures, they can be marked alternatively by force duration or pitch variation; sometimes, indeed, by all three at once.

In testing an example, the whole poem from which it is taken should be read; the spirit of a poem governs the nature of all the technical details of its interpretation.

CONTENTS

THE
SPEAKING OF ENGLISH VERSE

CHAPTER I

THE DISTINCTION BETWEEN PROSE AND VERSE

WHEN M. Jourdain appreciated with stupefaction the fact that he had all his life been speaking prose, he grasped part of the distinction which exists and must always exist between prose and verse: that in prose we concern ourselves chiefly with setting forth our meaning as simply and clearly as possible, while in verse we express ourselves, our feeling and emotion as well as our logical meaning, through a metric pattern of words.

Directly we have thus stated the difference, limitations and exceptions force themselves upon us. Prose can be as rhythmically beautiful as verse.

Some of the most magnificent prose in the world has been written in entire unconsciousness of beauty of style, with no other object than to be understood by the vulgar. But other prose writers, after "playing the sedulous ape" to their forerunners, have achieved with great effort an equal simplicity and directness coupled with so musical and individual a cadence that we seem to hear the author thinking aloud.

In significance prose can be as sublime as the

sublimest poetry, as stirring as a ballad, as passionate as a sonnet.

There is a path which no fowl knoweth and which the vulture's eye hath not seen. The lion's whelps have not trodden it, nor the fierce lion passed by it. He putteth forth his hand upon the rock; he overturneth the mountains by the roots.

.   .   .   .

But where shall wisdom be found, and where is the place of understanding? Man knoweth not the price thereof, neither is it found in the land of the living.

(Job xxviii. 4.)

"The sea," cried the Miller, "Lord help us all, it is the greatest thing God made! That is where all the water in the world runs down into a great salt lake. There it lies as flat as my hand, and as innocent-like as a child; but they do say when the wind blows it gets up into water-mountains bigger than any of ours, and swallows down great ships, bigger than our mill, and makes such a roaring that you can hear it miles away upon the land. There are great fish in it five times bigger than a bull, and one old serpent as long as our river and as old as all the world, with whiskers like a man, and a crown of silver on her head."

(R. L. Stevenson.)

It is not, then, content or the presence or absence of rhythm that distinguishes verse from prose.

In verse itself we may find free forms which to the eye conform to no strict and ordered pattern. There are others, like the ode, where only by going back over the printed page which is the record of the sounds of speech can we make out the pattern of the whole, a pattern in which the repetitions occur at such long distances from one another that we cannot through the ear alone carry its shape clearly enough in our mind.

The Greeks made the structure of such poems visible
through dancing and so showed forth their patterns.

How should we deal with modern free verse? Are
we to class it as prose or verse?

When lìlacs làst in the doòryard blòom'd,
And the great stàr early droòp'd in the western sky in
    the nìght,
I moùrn'd, and yet shall moùrn with èver-retùrning sprìng.
Ever-returning sprìng, trinity sùre to mè you brìng,
Lìlac bloòming pèrennial, and droòping stàr in the wèst,
And thòught of hìm I lòve.

WALT WHITMAN.

But at the last, when all this has been allowed for,
we still come back to the definition that verse, even
the freest verse, implies the presence of a fixed rhythmic
pattern, and that in prose we have free rhythm, not
seeking as part of its intention to produce rhythmic
patterns at all, but nevertheless—when it is good—full
of rhythm, because rhythm is a thing so much deeper
than metre, so inseparable from movement, that to
neglect it is to neglect the fundamental law of speech.

There is no word so misused, no conception about
which people mystify and bewilder themselves more
than this of rhythm. It is visible in dancing, where
it passes before our eyes in time. It is audible in poetry
or in music, in the beat of a perfectly-running engine.
It is visible again in sculpture and in painting, where
it lies spread before us in space, freed from the change
and obliteration of time, or reduced to its simplest
elements in decoration or pattern. It sings to us in
our own veins and in the pulse of life in our hearts,
telling us of health and disease, of joy or passion or
fear. The planets swing to it in their path round the
sun, the tides and the stars obey it. It can be only
a very simple and very essential thing to be of so

B

all-pervading a validity. I believe it to be, in fact, as simple and as essential as that force to which we give the name of gravity. I believe it to be our way of apprehending the fundamental law of movement, as gravity is our way of apprehending the fundamental law of stability.

Utterance consists of audible movement. Even those who most perfectly interpret what they silently read to themselves, do so, one must remember, solely through their muscular memory of the movements of audible speech. We have no other memory of words.

To train ourselves to the performance of these movements, and to their perfect control in the interpretation of verse, is therefore one means of deepening our own love and understanding of the medium of poetry.

The printed content of a book of verse is not only a record of significant words, it is the record of audible movements translated by visible signs. To appreciate verse we have to train ourselves to translate these signs mentally back again into sound-patterns without for an instant losing the verbal significance of the words themselves.

In reading easy prose we often make short cuts; a child will speak words it sees without thought of meaning, concentrating on

Sight = Sound.

A business man will read the City article without ever feeling that the signs he sees stand for any form of sound; they have become to him almost as conventional as the "Ideographs" of Chinese writing.

The writer who thinks only of the actual utterance of his poem is almost like the artist who "sees paint"; his work is valueless as art. But the poet who does not hear his verse and test it, as Wordsworth, for instance, did, with unwearied musical repetition, loses just that simplicity which is the note of all true folk-poetry, a simplicity which is present in all the great poems made before visible records were generally accepted; above all in the plays of our Shakespeare, who more than any poet made his verse for its appeal to the ear through speech, hardly troubling himself, through the whole of his lifetime, about the preservation of its written record.

In the art of making or speaking poetry the first place must therefore be given to a sense of the essential meaning of rhythm as a law of audible movement.

Every movement must pass through some portion of space, must occupy some interval of time, must be accomplished by some degree of force. The right measure of these things depends entirely on the intention of the movement. When space, time and force are all rightly measured under the exact guidance of intention the action which results is said to be rhythmical.

It is, however, necessary to define a little more completely what is meant by intention.

A block of stone rolling from the side of a cliff till its progress is arrested by the law of gravitation, represents a purely mechanical movement. The movements induced by growth and life, above all the movements of human action, give us inevitably the sense of intention. This is the case, though one cannot here attempt to explain it, even in the most elementary movements of organic growth, but the intention they suggest is not their own. They appear to us as the plastic material following out what we term "Natural Law." We are still blindly at a loss in the effort to explain many such natural phenomena, particularly when we come to the higher organisms, the profound

instincts of insects and birds, but in our own minds we
believe ourselves conscious of a purpose in action. We
pass through the animal stage of accommodation to
environment more slowly than any young animal, but
with a result which, to our own perceptions at least,
appears to open to us an infinity of choice in action.

The entire growth of consciousness during the first
years of child life practically concerns itself with nothing
but the solution of this problem. To direct the actions
of the neuro-muscular system through the brain centres
so that they shall synchronise space, time and force
in the service of a definite intention, this is in reality
the earliest education of every individual. To clutch,
to move, to reach, to walk, to speak—what are all
these activities but the development in rhythmic direction of the power of the neuro-muscular system? Always
the governing factor is the intention of the action
performed; always the instinct for its performance is
along the line of least resistance, the easiest, most
balanced, most definite performance; always the training progresses from the rough sketch of action, the
clumsy, uncontrolled, ill-directed, simple curve, to the
finished, balanced, correlated action which completely
expresses the practical intention of the agent. From
the hesitating stumble of the baby to the magic of
the dancer and the prowess of the athlete; from the
first lisped iteration of syllables to the eloquence of
the orator and the enthralling art of the great singer,
the pathway lies along one continuous channel, the
growth of rhythmic expression. Nor is there any
doubt that the primitive value of this rhythmic expression lies close to the very foundations of being.
The rhythmic action of mechanism is perceptible to
the trained ear in the music of its humming vibration,
to the trained eye in the smoothness of its working; in

the absence of heat, friction, fault of function. These things indicate in the mechanism perfection of construction and maintenance with adequate application of force. Error in space, by so small a fraction as the intrusion of a grain of grit; error in time, by the fraction of a second; error in force, by the over or under charging of the mechanism; all these result in progressive failure and ultimate destruction. And rhythmic action of the living organism indicates, in an infinitely more subtle but equally unmistakable manner, perfection of construction and maintenance with adequate application of force, the whole conditioned this time, not by one unvarying intention, but by the constant ebb and flow of choice, thought and feeling, which subserves the inner life of every individual.

The complexity of civilised existence takes up the greater part of this faculty of choice. We become absorbed in occupational training, sometimes in mere living, according to the code of an exacting and intolerant social, economic or religious standard; but we constantly seek escape in the direction of freedom of action. Sport, games, above all art, and the mystical and devotional elements of religion, are our avenues to such freedom.

By them, in ways excessively simple or incredibly complex, we seek for freedom of choice and expression, but by a curious antinomy are dissatisfied with it unless it is intensified and, as it were, pointed by harmony with chosen order and rule. The artist demands from life a measure of choice denied to other men and gives up material aims for self-realisation; the saint is content to forgo all worldly freedom to obtain the Pearl of Great Price, the Divine Comrade he has chosen for his soul. So self-expression becomes no longer simple as in the joyous frolicking of a young unbroken creature, but infinitely complex, and at times exquisitely torturing; yet always it keeps this character: we must do what we intend, we must "play the game," we must "realise our ideals," we must master the obstacles which our lower nature imposes on the higher freedom of our desire.

So the intelligence and the emotion of man soar beyond the conditions of mere existence and rejoice in the joy of creating. He longs to repeat, to arrange, to stimulate movement and form. Once again rhythm provides the condition necessary for this higher self-expression. Elemental at first, it gives us the mere joy of rhythmic movement; so closely connected with healthful activity of any kind that it can hardly be distinguished from the instinctive satisfaction of an accomplished impulse. Then by degrees it becomes self-conscious: the multitude of intentions takes on order, arrangement, spacing, above all recurrence, and their results express these more and more fully. So the various art forms are born, as rhythmic patterns are used, to express delight in movement:

(1) Movements giving patterns of action and gesture in dancing or miming.

(2) Movements giving patterns of rhythmic sound in music.

(3) Movements giving patterns of spoken or imagined words in poetry.

(4) Movements giving patterns of line, form and colour in the pictorial arts.

(5) Movements giving patterns of mass construction and balance in the plastic arts.

In the last two the artistic result is achieved in the record of the movement, not by movement itself, while the patterns presented to us most frequently convey the impression of movement arrested in time. We do not watch a painter's or a sculptor's movements, we watch the result that grows under his touch.

Fra Pandolph's hands worked busily a day. And there
    she stands.[1]

Much confusion exists between these patterns and the rhythm that creates them. Many people mistake time in music or metre in poetry for rhythm.

Many fail to see that all rhythm is movement, that speech, for instance, is movement: they think that when we speak of speech or song as movement, we mean that they should be accompanied by movement or gesture, or that we mean the beat and flow of the verse calling up images of movement to our minds.

They do not realise that all artistic training on the technical side is a training in rhythmic movement.

The foundation of all artistic expression is thought in action.

This is true even of the pictorial and plastic arts which achieve their own record in space during performance.

Every form of movement springs from a mental impulse. Long before specialised artistic training, except perhaps in dancing, can be given, the fundamental rhythmic control of the brain should be growing— that is, the capacity for measuring and synchronising space, duration and force under the immediate impulse of intention.

In the growth of every art there takes place a development from the stage when the delight in pattern is almost self-sufficing to that when the characteristic medium of the art has been brought entirely into subjection and free rhythm completely interprets intention.

According to the level of complexity at which we aim is the possibility of attaining this expression with

[1] *My Last Duchess.* R. Browning.

immediate spontaneity; though paradoxically we do not feel that the expression which is totally and absolutely spontaneous, irresistible, unconscious is so truly self-expressive as that in which we completely achieve our intention after practice and preliminary effort. The great artist who in a few strokes of sepia gives us the masterpiece of a Japanese drawing has behind him not merely a lifetime of observation and execution which produced the sureness of movement essential to express his own artistic meaning, but even centuries of preceding study and convention, accepted and rejected, in that study of artistic vocabulary which has been the dominant feature of Japanese art, as mastery of medium has been the dominant feature of Western art.

Now when we speak of intentional movement or of rhythmic movement as requiring intention, we do not necessarily mean we are thinking about, and voluntarily performing, that special movement—quite the contrary; we mean that particular movement is fulfilling to perfection its part in carrying out the whole action we wish to accomplish; and to do this, we must have a body flexible and alert to our will—often, indeed, we must have a body trained to the most extraordinary submission to our will. The great orator is not considering how he is to move his lips and tongue in order to articulate—they obey him, and carry out his intention by long practice or natural aptitude,—but the stammerer thinks of nothing else but those very movements which should be unconscious, and so destroying his own intention, becomes unrhythmic and finally unco-ordinated.

The art of poetry is, up to the present, our most complete illustration of the nature and value of rhythmic expression. Based on man's faculty of speech, its primitive development is lost to us in the dawn of the history of our race. It was in the form of folk song, war song, occupational lilt, ceremonial and ritual chaunt, that music—the art of non-significant rhythms—and the true poetry of significant words, developed together, and with the dawn of literary history we see the deliberate selection of the various elements of rhythm to form the basis of poetic patterns.

The development of time or quantity in accordance with the natural music of Greek speech gave us the complex variety of perfect classical metres.

The development of accent and the rigid accentual rhythms of early European literature, first into liberty of form, then into stress rhythm actually based upon the speech stresses of ordinary speech, have given us a variety which no purely mechanical pattern ever achieved.

The historic study of these forms will show us the true value of rhythmic development in the art of poetry, the impossibility of dividing form and meaning in any true artistic expression, and on them we can base a reasoned theory for the practice of verse-speaking.

CHAPTER II

MUSIC AND POETRY

In this study of spoken verse it will often be necessary to compare the arts of music and of poetry, since both depend for their existence on the power of making patterns from sound.

Yet no two arts are more fundamentally different in character. They are so different that they can be used as complementary one to the other. We can set a poem to music or write words to a tune which delights us. The difference touches both medium and content.

In music the fundamental basis of the art is found in a series of single colourless tones which we call notes. Their only fixed and determined quality is difference in pitch. Each note can be shortened or lengthened, stressed or lightened at will, but the pitch of each note must be definite and constant during its whole life. But for this distinction of pitch all music would be like the beating of a single drum, without harmony or melody.

These notes are grouped into series entirely based on their absolute or related pitch, *i.e.* on the harmony between certain rates of vibration. From this grouping we get scales in determined keys, chords and counterpoint. These form the units of musical art, and they possess no logical meaning whatever in themselves; they simply translate into sound one element of rhythmic movement. The single notes which form a melody are in themselves more colourless than the letters of

the alphabet, less charged with emotion than the palette
an artist prepares for his picture; they can be identified
when they stand alone only by those possessing the
gift of absolute pitch. Their upward and downward
limits are like the lines of the spectrum determined by
science, not by any artistic choice. Like the colours
of the rainbow they were discerned, noted and measured
by the artist centuries before the scientist discovered
in them the fundamental principle of sound. In music,
then, pitch is the fixed element of each note; the
duration and force are variable and must be specially
indicated.

Within our minds we think of the notes of the musical
scale as ranged in order like numbers, or like the colours
of the spectrum, and the thread of a single melody
to our ear passes from grade to grade among them,
touching or missing one or another, tracing a delicate
arabesque of pattern. There are points where the order
of the notes makes, as it were, a bridge of sound carrying
us smoothly from one series to another, and we accept
a change of key. If it takes place roughly, we feel the
sequence broken and our ear is jarred.   When the
design is accomplished the impression left on our mind
is that of a spacial pattern. If we reinforce it by difference in the force with which the different grades
are attained, and by difference in the period during
which each grade of sound is presented to our ear, we
have the three elements of rhythm—space, time, force
—present in our pattern.

When "parts" or harmonies built up out of "parts"
are sung, we have a series of patterns crossing and
intercrossing in the grades or sequences of musical pitch
like geometric design, till at last, in the crash and
sonority of a great orchestra we seem to feel the per-
spectives of some architectural design, one line of

tone-pattern fading out and vanishing behind another
to reappear at its appointed moment, one material
superimposed upon another, and we ourselves seem to
stand within the great sphere of sound, not merely to
watch it pass before us like the rhythm of a Greek frieze.

What is the unit of poetry? Just occasionally the
poet may use a refrain built from meaningless syllables;
even then, we quickly make some association of meaning
with their sound. With this solitary exception, he
has for his material, instead of the pure, colourless,
flexible material of musical notes, the words and phrases
of human speech.

Words charged with logical and emotional significance,
full of the most personal associations, not only to the
poet himself but to his hearers. Every line of verse he
makes out of these words must satisfy not only the
demands of logical meaning and metric form, but
numberless grammatical and logical associations which
we call rules. Most of those who read his verse will
be thinking first of the logical meaning of his words
and the emotional feeling called up by the subject of
the poem, and will be annoyed if the pattern which
delights him "gets in the way" of the plain meaning
of a sentence, or prevents the reader from letting
his feelings run away with him under the emotional
appeal of the subject.

Just recently, a young Englishman, much interested
in the theatre and its concerns, told me how much
he preferred hearing Shakespeare in the French prose
translation, because he so disliked "the jigging sing-
song of the lines."

It is almost impossible to measure the extent and
the profundity of our unconscious association with
words. Pictures, perfumes, passionate memories, instinctive repulsions, hateful vulgarities, soaring en-

thusiasms, they call up all these for us without thought of their bare logical significance.

Take the word which is the theme of Stevenson's lines quoted on page 2: "The sea."

To those who are blessed with the magic background of Greek thought and art, it cries "Thalassa! Thalassa!" with Xenophon's legion or calls up Poseidon and Athene striving for the soul of Athens; all Venice in her witchery sweeps past us as we read of the city

> Where the Doges used to wed the sea with rings.

It strikes us with intolerable pain as we remember it stained by the cruelty and hate of men.

To the scientist it calls up the struggle for life at its lowest depth of inhumanity. The hope of ultimate reunion with those we love has found no more perfect expression than this:

> And there was no more sea.

Till Kipling told us of the "silly sailor folk" to whom it meant the salt and sting of life, or Masefield sang:

> I must go down to the sea again . . .

to paint the wanderthirst which calls us, where lies

> Beyond the East the sunrise, beyond the West the sea.

To those who have known life or the magic reflection of the Golden Islands, some echo, some perfume of all this clings for ever to the word. Yet, the poem may be read by a young lady to whom it suggests the parade, with its bathing-boxes and troupes of pierrots.

Consider again the degradation in the level of vocabulary which befalls certain words; a childish and amusing instance appears in the desperate choice which lies before the English poet seeking his rhyme for that quintessential word: "Love."

How early Shakespeare disregarded the trite

> " Pronounce but love and dove."

even in favour of the poor expedient of the eye-rhyme
"remove" or "prove"! But who could be so daring
as to venture "shove"! even though its logical meaning
be no more unpoetical than "heave":

> . . . May heave his head
> From golden slumber on a bed
> Of heap'd Elysian flowers.

Such considerations as these give us a keen sense of
the essential difference of medium in music and in
poetry. This fundamental difference of medium serves
above all to direct our attention to a still more profound
difference of content. Music is not required to give us
any suggestion or imitation of natural objects as painting
and sculpture commonly do. It is more independent
than the equally abstract art of decorative design. It
does not serve as a logically constructed language,
which, however we may purify it of discordant associations, affects us through our knowledge, our association,
our grasp of words.

We are not absurd if we require of the most perfect
poetry that its subject and associations shall be sublime,
significant, and related to what we call truth.

We are conscious that to ask of music that it shall
in itself call up definite logical meanings to our mind
is to lower its artistic perfection. It should be self-
sufficing. When we require of it this definiteness of
logical meaning we realise it should be achieved not
by torturing its forms into an exaggerated onomatopœia,
but in harmonies

> Married to immortal verse

in such forms as music-drama, or great choral or single-voiced singing, where words supply the missing link with logical thought. So great music remains independent of time, place, race or age in a way to which no other art can attain. It needs no "translation" and it bridges differences of creed and social organisation by appealing to abstract beauty of form and to an indescribable correspondence between sound-pattern and emotion.

We must now recognise the points of resemblance in the structure and appeal of the two arts with equal clearness in order to understand the true difficulty of poetic diction and the art of verse-speaking.

Difference and resemblance alike are shown in their respective use of the three elements of time, force and space in rhythm.

Pitch, the distinctive element of music, is heard in European music as pure and sustained sound at a definite rate of vibration, it shifts neither up nor down except in definite and measured degrees. We are conscious of these degrees as if they were set before us in a series, in determined order, much as we are conscious of the ordered degrees of number. We speak of this order as going "up" or "down," and we are conscious of it as moving in that manner through a musical plane which affects the ear very much as space affects the eye.

When we turn to the musical instruments which give us a definite notation we find that they strengthen this mental impression of a spacial movement in pitch variation, since in practice nearly all of them are constructed to give us pitch variation as a result of spacial movement on some surface. We are obliged to construct them with a keyboard or a series of strings or stops or frets and to arrange their mechanism so that the movements required to play them are always spacial movements. We vary force in movement so as to express accent, we vary successive duration and speed to measure time, but when we wish to produce pitch variation we make a movement in space right or left, up or down. We tend therefore to be conscious of pitch as musical space. So the marking of accent depends on a training in the regulation of the force of our movements, the marking of time on a training in regulating the speed of our movements, and the playing of the right notes on a spacial training in reaching the right point of the string or keyboard. And we rightly insist that in order to be of any musical value all this training must be done through the ear, and through the ear alone, no matter what other aids we may afterwards employ, since in the ear alone where sound is concerned lies the criterion of intention—the test of whether the action required has been rhythmically performed, *i.e.* synchronising force, time and space under the direction of intention.

To see this a little more clearly play on the piano a rhythm of nine notes divided into three by a marked accent on every third note. You will find you have touched the same spot again and again with your finger, and made an ugly monotonous little pattern by measuring the degree of force only with which your finger strikes the note:

$$\overset{>}{\rho}\ \rho\ \rho\ \overset{>}{\rho}\ \rho\ \rho\ \overset{>}{\rho}\ \rho\ \rho$$

Now repeat this, holding one note in three and stressing as little as you can. You will like this pattern much better, and you will find you have made it by a change in the timing of each movement:

Now make your pattern by raising the pitch of every third note, and you will find you must at once make a spacial movement left or right in order to carry out your intention. If you do not make it accurately you will blur between two notes and lose the right pitch change:

But there is another element in musical sound which needs very careful understanding. We hear a musical note and recognise it more or less accurately (relatively at all events): we say it is "high" or "low." But this sound which we hear as one impression has in it really a number of pitches blended together. Picture to yourself a little basin of smooth polished marble shaped to a perfect curve and filled with pure water. Imagine that at its exact centre you drop a little glass ball very gently and smoothly. A circle will run to the edge of the basin, and at regular intervals others will follow it in an unbroken pattern. So would you have a single series of pitch vibrations dying as the impulse which produced them failed. The nearest we come to such a sound is the note of a tuning-fork. Now watch the ripple strike against the sides of the basin, and immediately other ripples will fly back from these to the centre again in a contrary direction, crossing and intersecting the first, and making a beautiful pattern on the surface of the water. This illustrates very roughly the phenomenon we all know as resonance. The shape, texture, tension and surface of the resonator will each vary the strength and speed and intensity of these returning waves and the angles at which they return, and from these slighter, more broken, less constant waves—"harmonics," as they are called—will

c

result the "quality" of the final sound that reaches our ear.

Now suppose that the resonator consists not of one chamber, but of three or more opening one from the other; the shape of the resulting resonances will give us a series of curious sound-patterns, differing very markedly one from the other. Wake them with a wave of sound not strong enough to disturb or break them up, and you will have what we now call a vowel. In the case of the human voice you have your resonator so delicately balanced and formed that you can wake them with a breath alone, with what we call a whisper, and if you whisper them in their musical order quickly, one after another, choosing only the clearest and most varied, you will be able to hear for yourself that they are made of pitches blended together into a characteristic note, so:

oo   oh   aw   ah   eh   ee.

If, on the other hand, you say them aloud, you will find that you have drowned their delicate essential pitch vibration with the dominant pitch vibration and resonances of the organ of the voice, the larynx. You will hear the vowel quality, but its pitch will be merged in that of whatever voice note you have formed. If this is carelessly or roughly done the quality of the vowel itself becomes affected.

This is the foundation of the art of song: a series of musical pitches, exactly spaced and measured to what we call a scale, sounding through a resonator shaped to give a particular succession of vowel qualities just as exactly measured and sustained. Presently we shall see how in speech these two elements become less and less exactly measured: pitch, the musical element, gliding up and down the scale much more inexactly, and with a smaller range, the vowel sounds asserting their peculiar quality and duration more and more strongly against the musical element and forming in poetry the subtle music of vowel succession, of assonance and of rhyme. The elements of friction contained in what we call consonants, divide and group and "articulate" the sound in both song and speech, producing the sound-groups which make up our words, and so making possible our vocabulary, our sentence structure, and the whole body of logical and emotional speech by which we express ourselves.

Music and song, poetry, free verse rhythms, prose, ordinary speech, these give us a series of rhythms in which ordered pattern plays a less and less important part; in which such patterns grow less and less self-sufficing, the elements of logical convention grow stronger and stronger, till they overcome significant form altogether and all sense of art is lost. Yet because of the peculiar character of human speech, because of that association of thought and feeling with the spoken word, which I sketched above, this never absolutely takes place; music, poetry, song remain equally perfect as mediums for artistic expression, while hardly inferior to them are the prose rhythms where verbal felicity, based on meaning and association, may constantly compensate for an apparently less significant form.

Turn now to poetry. You will find that the fixed value of stress in words allows us to build definite verse-patterns based on accent. You will not be able to hear so clearly that there are patterns based on duration, because when you try to hear these, you will not always easily distinguish in ordinary pronunciation which words have a long duration and which a short. And also because we have allowed ourselves the stupid habit of calling a vowel "long" or "short" to indicate a varying quality, without taking the slightest trouble to measure with our ear whether it is long or short in actual duration. But if you will read aloud some lines of a very perfect poem, you will find that one of the most beautiful effects in it is obtained by holding the duration of a vowel sound or of a syllable for a longer or shorter period. Always provided that this does not spoil the natural way of speaking the word and that the one sound actually takes perceptibly longer to make than the others, as the vowel sound of "pine" in ordinary speech takes twice as long to make as the vowel sound of "pit."

And you will recognise a great many difficult things: for instance that a word of one syllable like "in, "with," "by," "it," has no inevitable accent of its own, but only the accent which belongs to its meaning in the sentence. That many words can be long or short in quantity according to their meaning.[1] And so you will find that meaning not only governs absolutely the choice of words for verse, but that the pattern determined by the logical sense of the sentence must be considered in making the verse-pattern, otherwise the tune of the verse will sound sing-song and stupid, like a child counting the 3/4 beats of a valse in strict time.

But it is when you come to the element of space that you will meet the greatest difficulty of all. For English words have practically no fixed pitches whatever. You may think for a moment that the syllable which is stressed in a word is always a little higher in pitch than the one which is unaccented, but directly you put the word into a sentence you will find that this tiny difference is drowned by a much louder pitch-difference, due to some special kind of

[1] See Chapter V., verse examples.

meaning in your voice, which changes a whole phrase into an upward or downward scale.

Here we have one reason for the poet's dislike of overmuch rise or fall in pitch in the delivery of verse.

He has no means of indicating the pitch he requires as he can indicate stress and quantity. Still more: exaggerated and chaunted delivery on the one hand, and colloquial or conventional delivery on the other, tend to weaken, and even to obliterate, the essential values of the vowel sounds themselves, and so, as these vowel elements form the true fixed spacial values of words, tend to drown their sound-significance—what Newbolt so well calls "the sound of the sense." This difficulty will have to be dealt with more in detail later. For the moment it is only necessary to show its connection with the essential distinctions of speech and song.

We may take it then that vowel quality, rhyme assonance and vowel succession form the true spacial element of poetry and that the training required for speaking begins in the perfect formation of the musical resonances of the vowels—the relation of lip and tongue movement to voice; that we obtain sense of stress by the varying force of our articulatory movements and the degree of loudness or softness in our vocal tones on individual syllables. Finally that we mark quantity or duration by our power of sustaining or checking vowel sound, and lengthening or shortening the time employed in forming the successive movements required to shape a syllable. The great importance of pure and musical vowel quality in the art of verse-speaking now becomes clear, and the fact that far more than a bare phonetic standard of accuracy is necessary.

From these considerations we may deduce three principles:

i. Vowel quality is the melody of verse and takes the place of great pitch-variety in the speaking of verse, particularly in lyric verse where it is pointed by assonance and rhyme.

ii. Quality itself being the result of blended pitches and of vowels possessing essential pitch affinities of their own, the best way of gaining the sense of pure vowel quality is through sung practice at clear musical pitches, more definite than can be obtained in speech.

iii. In order to make this practice of real value, song and speech should be studied as one in the early stages of training. Song purifies vocal tone by sustaining and clarifying pitch and stabilising quality.

CHAPTER III

THE HISTORY OF VERSE PATTERNS

In the three examples on page 2 three different ways of marking sound-rhythms are indicated.

But it is clear that the three elements in them are not of equal importance.

With a little pains it is possible to play No. 2 so that there will be no element of varying power or accent in it.

No. 3 can be played so that there will be no difference of duration in the individual notes, and no difference of force or accent.

But there is one thing which must be present before there can be any sense of pattern whatever, and that is some element of regular succession of the pattern chosen in time.

I use this word here not in its musical but in its logical sense, the sense in which we speak of "time passing."

This is really a very simple fact. No one will deny that all the patterns we can see, whether decorative or expressive, must be patterns in space. Colour, line or mass, painting, sculpture, decorative art—all these are conceived and executed in definite relation to space. They divide, emphasise, decorate, occupy space. They remain before us spread out or built up in space; we can go back and receive their total impression at one moment in space. If their relation to space were confused or non-significant we should not recognise them as patterns at all. Where they use the element of repetition it is to emphasise their relation to space,

25

and to make the nature of their spacial design more clear by repeating it.

In dancing we have a double pattern. We have first the spacial design present before our eyes at any moment, the silhouette of the dance, its grouping or posing or mass formation—the instantaneous photograph, as it were, taken at any single moment in the dance.

But more than this we have the pattern which is the result of the course of the dance from its beginning to its end, a succession of poses or steps incessantly changing one into the other at given rates of speed. To control this order with its time-patterns, its succession and climaxes we use music. And here we notice that repetition is necessary if we are to have any clear perception of the order of the pattern; because this does not remain before us at any moment in its entirety as a set, motionless, spacial pattern does. We have no fixed record of the dance as a whole which we can look at; it is only when we see a movement repeated that we can form any clear idea through memory of its complete order. The movement-pattern must be a pattern in time.

So with audible movement, with speech and its use in the art of poetry. These things pass through our mind in time; their audible patterns are time-patterns. Unless they divide, emphasise or decorate the passage of time they are meaningless to us as patterns. If their basis is accent, we must hear those accents or stresses recurring at definite intervals in time; if they use variety of duration or quantity as their basis we must hear the length-waves during some regular interval of time, our ear must expect and recognise them, and the pattern must very constantly repeat, at very short intervals, so that we may hear and identify it, recognise its beginning, climax and end. Recurrence in time, of the selected elements of a pattern, becomes the basic feature of musical or metric structure.

Again we must make it clear that here, too, rhythm can exist without forming regular pattern and therefore without actual recurrence. Prose can be majestically rhythmical, can give us the sensation of growth and movement under the direction of intention. But we cannot anticipate its cadences, and their significance altogether dominates and dwarfs their verbal music. Visual patterns then are seen as displayed in space; time in them is reduced to the result of a single momentary impression. Audible movement is heard in succession as it flows past us in time.

Dancing uses both time and space.

Time being more difficult to measure than space since it flows past us irretrievably, repetition forms a stronger element in audible than in visual patterns, except in those of dancing.

In the visual arts again, the work of the artist or of the sculptor is its own record. In music or in poetry a mechanical record must be made afterwards, and it need not be in any sense a work of art. No adequate means of making a record of the double appeal of dancing has yet been found.

The cinema's failure [1] in this direction serves to make plainly evident its lack of rhythm in action.

How can a pattern be made in sounds that have a logical meaning?

    i. By marking the duration of the vowel sounds or of the actual syllables sounded; the longer or shorter sounds sustained and recurring at regular intervals of time.

        This is called quantity.

[1] The cinema film cannot yet record rapidly enough to give more than a series of momentary interrupted pictures reducing the screen movements to a series of unrhythmical jerks.

ii. By marking certain syllables or words with a greater force of articulation or loudness of voice. These accents or stresses recurring at regular intervals, and sometimes with a regular number only of unstressed syllables between them.

This is called accent or stress.

iii. By arranging words so that the higher pitch sounds in them will recur at regular intervals of time and make a tune or tone-pattern.

No European language now bases prosody on this form, though it had a marked place in Greek verse.

iv. By marking the varying qualities of certain vowels and the likeness and difference of certain consonants and arranging the recurrence of similar sounds at regular intervals.

Assonance, alliteration, rhyme. This fourth element adds a musical beauty to song as well as to speech.

The particular element which we select to form the basis of verse patterns is not a matter of arbitrary choice. It is determined absolutely and instinctively by the genius of the language in which the poem is written.

There is some idea that Latin verse formed an exception to this rule. It is far more probable that it registered a change, a refinement which was actually taking place in the language, at a time when conscious analysis of metric form became general, and when Greek influence was training the ear to a distinction of fine shades of duration in vowel sound—a matter which is more easy of modification than the fixed stress syllables of words.

It seems at least probable that English verse is being

spoken with a greater regard for quantity at the present time than in the days, say, of Pope, if we are to judge by the extraordinary confusion in nomenclature and in definition found in the critics from the beginning of the second half of the eighteenth century up to a few years ago.

Take this comical illustration from a nursery rhyme:

" Dickory Dickory Dock, the Mouse ran up the clock."

We should like

Dìck ŏ rў |Dìck ŏ rў |Dòck ‖ thĕ Mōuse |r͞a͞n |ŭp thĕ clòck. |

better than

Dìck ŏ rў |Dìck ŏ rў |Dòck ‖ thĕ Moùse |ran ùp |thĕ clòck

The first marks the duration of the successive syllables and vowels and sets the pattern in time.

The second jigs out the accents and makes no attempt to mark the time-divisions with any variety.

It is the first which brings out most clearly the sense stress of the lines.

Of course in a nonsense verse we prefer that the pattern should be fantastic and ridiculously metric. It adds the sound to the nonsense. Just as in serious verse we want the sound of the sense: significant pattern.

Greek—which gives us the first example of known prosody in Europe—used the natural individuality of its time-rhythms and gave us metric patterns founded on quantity and traversed by more or less fixed pitch-variations.

This is because classic Greek was a Tone language, a language in which the fixed pitch of a word distinguished its meaning, as emphasis brings out the exact meaning of a word in English. Stress seems to have

been almost foreign to the genius of Greek speech. As
it is to-day to French verse, where little French children
instinctively chaunt:

Pe - tit en - fant de-jà la brume ‖ s'é - lève au fond de la va-llée

while little English children saw out their imaginary
iambics:

> How dòth | the *lìt* | tle bù | sy bèe | . . .
> De lìght | to bàrk | and bìte |
> And gà | thers hòn | ey àll | the dày | . . .
> And grùbbs it ùp | at nìght. |

with no thought of anything but a succession of strong
and weak syllables.

But the Greeks not only, like all other peoples,
made patterns of words recognisable and measurable
to the ear in the natural tune of their speech,
later they discovered the actual principle on which
it was best to make such patterns and so established the
first definite rules of what is known as Prosody.

The first principle of this was the counting of syllables,
in order to secure as regular a succession as possible in
time for the long-held and short-held sounds which
constituted the striking difference on which their verse-
pattern was based.

These syllables, measured out, formed as it were the
time-signature of their verse. They examined the actual
structure of their language and found that when it was
spoken perfectly it gave three levels of duration in its
vowel sounds. One long,
                    One short,
                    One intermediate:

the last by a little pulling or clipping being made long

or short. They then discerned that certain syllables took so long to pronounce, because of a combination of consonants which could be dwelt on by the voice, with vowels not in themselves long—that they allowed for syllabic as well as vowel quantity, and called the vowels in these syllables "long by position." They found that certain syllables both in monosyllabic and dissyllabic words were always sounded higher or lower in pitch than others. This in the written language came to be marked by a little dash or stroke as we mark the stress of words, and to this is given what is to *us* the very misleading name of "accent," just as the French use the same sign to mark a difference in the quality of different vowel sounds indicated by the same letter, and call them "accent grave," "accent aigu," "accent circonflexe," though they have nothing to with what we mean by accent—namely, greater or less degree of force or loud ness in sounding a syllable. We ourselves say a person speaks with a cockney "accent" or has a good "accent" in speaking English or French when we do not mean that they merely stress their words rightly. And we use the word in yet another sense when we say:

> Her pitying accents smote his heart,

or

> In trembling accents he.

Therefore, during the rest of these notes the word "accent" will not be used unless its meaning is made doubly clear by the context, and the word "stress" will be used to indicate force or loudness in any particular word or syllable; and the word "emphasis" for the logical stressing of a word or sentence to bring out its full significance, a stress which may be accomplished in many different ways, but which has nothing to do with verse as such. The Greeks did not specifically consider stress in making their verse, probably because they marked difference of force in their words very lightly.

They then considered the natural way into which words of more than one syllable tended to group long and short sounds, and finding a very great variety they established a corresponding variety of metrical units or, as we say, "feet." A foot in verse means, in any language, the most natural groups into which the syllables fall in words.

Words of one syllable can be arranged according to their logical meaning. The prevailing time-beat of the verses must be fixed by words of more than one syllable. Words tend to keep their verbal unity. If we break a long word up between two feet the verbal unity of that word will tend to make the sense override the sound in that line. We shall see later how we sometimes delight in this and at other times dislike it, but when a language is very poor in words which naturally form some one kind of "foot" the number of poems written in that beat will tend to be small, and those in which it is used will not be very stable; they will tend to slip away into other forms. In English, for instance, we have very few words of three syllables stressed on the last as in

Lochinvàr, macaroòn, parakeèt.

So when we use that beautiful metre called by the name of a Greek foot "anapæstic," we "find it constantly tending to slip back into the much more usual so-called "dactylic" metre. Thus:

Oh Yoùng |Lochinvàr |is come oùt |of the wèst |
Through àll |the wide bòrder |his stèed |was the bèst |

becomes, if we follow verbal unity as we must in stress verse:

And sàve his |good bròadsword |he wèapon |had nòne |
He ròde |all unàrmed |and he ròde |all alòne. |

We therefore judge that duration or brevity of vowel and syllable sound was the thing that struck the ear most easily in listening to Hellenic Greek, that this was pointed and grouped by measured and fixed pitch-variations, and that out of these two elements it was possible to form easy natural groups called feet, which could become the basic figure or pulse-beat of different metres. It is essential to keep on guarding against the idea so common to metrists and grammarians that poets write to obey rules. It is as ridiculous as the view of the amateur that any string of syllables which can be squeezed or pulled out into a recognisable pattern is "verse" or even poetry!

The beginning of a poem is the passionate expression of an emotional experience in rhythmic words as spontaneous as a dance of joy or the headlong delight of a colt's gallop. But the finishing of a poem is the scrupulous soul-searching analysis of sense and of sound, the correction of every line by the standard of the inner beat of rhythmic pattern, felt almost as much as heard. Where this may fail, technical knowledge of verse-forms will and must supply the reason of the failure, and the means of searching out its remedy. But no poet is content when he is compelled to fall back on it. We may name, analyse, finger out his tunes; to himself they must have seemed as inevitable as the crystallisation pattern of a diamond or the structure of the exquisite flinty volutes of a diatom. His only conscious struggle was probably to select out of the torrent of words and figures that rushed in on him just those which departed least from the vision within his brain.

And the Greek was gifted (above all other people except ourselves) with this power of incarnating thought in spontaneous and exquisite music of words; he was fortunate not only in his emotional inspiration but in the vehicle through which it was conveyed.

Time marked by itself. By the duration of continuous waves of different length grouped by number and divided by silence as rhythmic as sound. Phrases reaching their climax by the rise and fall of musical pitch. This is in its essence a finer thing than time beaten out in a drum rhythm which sounds a gong to mark its passing but cannot take part in its movement. Those who have conceived of modern verse as having no other foundation than this are still in the tom-tom stage of musical appreciation.

How far is it possible to reconstruct the vanished music of Greek verse? The first step is to forget all the strange and weird exercises in so-called scansion which were associated with the routine classical education and to try and feel quantity as a matter of duration —a long vowel being held for twice the time of a short one and so on. This will not take us very far, but is a beginning.

Three passages of Greek verse have been spoken for the author by Dr. Rouse; two are reproduced in the following phonetic transcriptions.[1] These include a musical notation indicating the rhythmic pulse of the line as actually delivered, as well as the fundamental underlying beat or "scansion" of the metric pattern, and marking in so doing the long and short vowel sounds with lines of long and short duration. Finally the raised accentuated tone pitches are roughly indicated in the same way by a curve or line which rises above the level of the other notes in the stave.

[1] See also Chapter IV., page 100.

euíppuɪ   kséne   ,   tâɪsde   khóɪraɪs

híkuɪ   tá   krátista   gâɪs   épaula,

tón   argêɪta   koloɪnón,   énth

haɪ   lígeia   minýɪretai

thamídzuɪsa   málist   aɛɪdóɪn

khloɪrâis   hypó   bássais,

D

tón   oinɔipón   ékhuisa   kissón

kái   táin   ábaton   theûi

phylláda   myiriókarpon   anéilion

anéinemón   te   pántɔin

kheimóinɔin,   hín   ho   bakkhióitais

aéi   diónyisos   embatéuei

theâis   amphipolô:n   thé:nais.

â:r án par hy:mô:n, ô: ksénoi, máthoim hópu:

tá tû: tyránnu: dó:mat estín oidípu:;

málista d autón éipat, ei. kátisth hópu:.

stégai mén háide, kautós éndon, ô: ksène;

gyné: dé mé:te:r hé:de tô:n kéinu: téknɔ:n.

all olbíaı te kaí ksýn olbíois aéi

génoit, ekéinuı g ûısa panteléıs dámar.

áutɔıs dé kái sú g, ɔ̄ı ksén; áksios gár êi

têıs euepéias húınek. allá phrádz hótuı

khrêidzɔın aphíıksai khôı ti seımêınai thélɔın.

agathá dómois te kái pósei tôı sôı, gýnai.

tá pòia tâuta? pará tínos d aphigménos?

ek têιs korínthuι. tó d épos huιkserôι tákha,

héιdoio mén, pòιs d uιk án, askhállois d ísɔιs.

tí d ésti, póiaιn dýnamin hôιd ékhei diplêιn;

týrannon autón huιpikhóιrioi khthonós

têιs isthmíaιs stéιsuιsin, hɔιs εudâιt ekêi.

The character of the rhythm here indicated illustrates certain definite characteristics recorded by tradition in regard to Greek lyric and dramatic performances.

First that the musical accompaniment, chiefly that of flutes, was based as closely as possible on the actual musical "tune" of the spoken verse. This could be absolutely done in regard to quantity and stress, but it can be seen that the existence of determined pitch in words made it also possible in regard to pitch. Again, the nature of this very definite quantitative rhythm also explains the close association of dancing and poetry in choric art. The dances illustrated on the vases would be impossible to purely accentual rhythms with their lack of sustained phrasing. We can also understand the tradition of the laughter excited by the mistake of an actor who substituted γαλῆν (weasel) for γαλήν' (calm), the distinction between the two words being one of pitch. It would be possible for a Chinese actor to-day to make the same kind of mistake, since Chinese words depend for their meaning on the pitch at which their syllables are spoken. Finally we can understand that the audience could under these conditions give an absolutely musical attention to the metric structure of the verse, and hiss a "false quantity" as an Italian audience to-day would hiss a note sung out of time.

The need of rhyme in verse with so clear and melodic a structure would not be felt; the function of rhyme is so definitely melodic; phrasing the rhythm, and by its repetition developing the exact character of the pattern to the ear. But the varied grouping of quantity, marked to this extent, forms in itself a melodic unity which the drum-beat of accent does not achieve. One more point is of importance. The stanzaic forms of Greek verse, the ode and choric ode and dance songs, show a structure so elaborate and repetitions so exact, that they could be followed only with difficulty even in a written record. It is plain that when spoken it was their interpretation in danced, or as we should say, in mimed movements, that really made their structure apparent.

The strophe with the turn again,

as Browning calls it, was, in the traditional way of marking off strophe and antistrophe, something obviously very different from the mechanical drill evolutions, or the casual draped poses indulged in by certain modern revivals of classic drama. The nature of these movements is discussed more fully in connection with the history of poetic form in a later chapter.

The quantitative character of Latin verse is generally held to have been deliberately determined. It may not improbably have depended on a marked differentiation between literary diction and popular speech—a distinction much more comprehensible in Latin than in Greek art, and harmonising with the whole history of poetic form in Roman literature.

It may be owing to this deliberately literary diction that we become more conscious of the conflict between meaning and metre in Latin than in Greek verse.

A short phonetic transcript illustrates the delicate poise and fall of syllables in Latin verse. There are no pitch marks, as these have been irrecoverably lost with the spoken inflections of the language.

— — | — ⏑ ⏑ | — — | — — | — ⏑⏑ | — —
ɑt reː | giːnɑ grɑ | wiː jɑm | duːdun | sɑukiɑ | kuːrɑː

— ⏑ ⏑ | — — | — — | — — | — ⏑ ⏑ | — —
wɔlnus ɑ | lit weː | niːs, ɛt | kɑikoː | kɑrpitur | iŋniː.

— ⏑ ⏑ | — — | — ⏑ ⏑ | — — | — ⏑ ⏑ | — —
multɑ wi | riː wir | tuːs ɑni | moː, mul | tuskwɛ rɛ | kursɑt

_ ◡ ◡| _   _ | _   _ | _ _ | _ ◡ ◡ | _ _

gentis hɔ|noıs; haı|rɛnt in|fiksıı|pɛktɔrɛ|wɔltuıs

_ ◡ ◡ ◡| _   _   ◡◡| _   _ | _   ◡ ◡ | _   ◡   _|

wɛrbakwɛ,|nɛk plaki|dam mem|briıs dat|kuıra kwi|

_ _

eıtɛm.

pɔstɛra|foebeı|aı lus|traıbat|lampadɛ|tɛrraıs
uımɛn|tɛŋkwɛ_au|roıra pɔ|loı diı|moıwɛrat| umbram,
kun siık|uınani|mã_adlɔkwi|tur malɛ|saına sɔ|roırɛm:
anna sɔ|roır, kwaı|meı sus|pɛnsã_in|sɔmnia|tɛrrɛnt!
kwis nɔwus|hiık nɔs|triıs suk|kɛssit|seıdibus|hɔspɛs,
kwɛn seı|seı_oirɛ fɛ|rɛns, kwam|fɔrtiı|pɛktɔrɛ_ɛt|
armiıs!
kreıdoı_ɛkwi|dɛn, nɛk|waına fi|deıs, gɛnus|ɛssɛ dɛ|
oırum.
deıgɛnɛ|reıs ani|moıs timɔr|arguit.|heu, kwibus|illɛ
jaktaı|tus faı|tiıs! kwai|bɛlla_ɛks|hausta ka|neıbat!
siı mihi|noın ani|moı fik|sũ_inmoı|tuŋkwɛ sɛ|deırɛt,
neı kui|meı wiŋ|kloı wɛl|lɛm sɔki|aırɛ ju|gaıliı,
pɔstkwam|priımus a|moır deı|kɛptam|mɔrtɛ fɛ|fɛllit;
siı noın|pɛrtaı|sum thala|miı tai|daikwɛ fu|issɛt,
huik uı|niı fɔr|san pɔtu|iı suk|kumbɛrɛ|kulpai.
anna, fa|teıbor ɛ|nim, misɛ|riı pɔst|faıta sy|khaiı
kɔnjugis|ɛt spar|soıs fraı|tɛrnaı|kaidɛ pɛ|naıtis,
soılus hik|inflɛk|sit sɛn|suıs, ani|muŋkwɛ la|bantɛm
inpulit|adgnoı|skoı wɛtɛ|ris wɛs|tiıgia f|lammai.
sɛd mihi|wɛl tɛl|lus ɔp|tɛm prius|iıma dɛ|hiskat,
wɛl patɛr|ɔmnipɔ|tɛns adi|gat meı|fulminɛ_ad|um-
braıs,
pallɛn|tiıs um|braıs ɛrɛ|biı nɔk|tɛŋkwɛ prɔ|fundam,
antɛ, pu|doır, kwan|teı wiɔ|loı_aut tua|juıra rɛ|sɔlwoı.
illɛ mɛ|oıs, priı|mus kwiı|meı sibi|juŋksit a|moıreıs
apstulit;|illɛ_habɛ|at sẽ|kun sɛr|wɛtkwɛ sɛ|pulkroı
siık ɛf|faıta si|mul lakri|miıs in|pleıwit ɔb|ɔrtiıs.

VIRGIL, *Æneid IV*.

To what do we owe the complete disappearance of quantity as a basis for verse patterns before the dawn of modern European poetry? Three reasons are generally adduced:

i. The decline of pure poetic diction throughout the the Roman Empire with the incursion of the Barbarians and the growth of dialect forms.

This would account for a loss of all finer shades of distinction in vowel sound. Among all un-educated people quality and quantity of vowel sound become shifting and uncertain. Roughly-made verse always allows a barbarous irregularity of stress to fill out defective lines.

ii. The setting of new words to old and familiar tunes where, so long as the notes and syllables could be fitted together, the value of the musical notes covered up all divergence of quantity.

Robert Bridges suggests that the octosyllabic church hymns may have been the first step in this direction, pointing out that as these hymns were sung to tunes generally of equal notes with a tendency to equal alternate stress, they tended to bring about that alternate stress which is the "norm and bane" of syllabic verse.

iii. The influence of two new elements in Keltic and Teutonic verse-patterns.

Assonance and vowel chiming in the first and alliteration with strong stress-pattern in the second.

The first may be held responsible for the complete loss of the tradition of true quantitative patterns.

Of the second I am a little more doubtful. It coincides with the gradual divorce between music and poetic form, and at most it seems to have prevented a survival of quantity in the church services where barbarous influences would probably have destroyed it in any case.

The last, again, simply reflects the national genius of the new languages as quantity reflected that of the Mediterranean tongues. In Keltic assonance a system of the most incredible complexity recalls the exquisite cord patterns of their illumination and of their almost microscopic silver, gold and copper work. Considering the evolution of verse-pattern we can say that the element of vowel quality, a form of pitch or spacial pattern, and the easy going kinetic rhythm of stress-patterns felt with the muscles of the body in war song or bardic story, become the genuine basis of the modern European verse-patterns before the dawn of modern poetry.

One element must not be neglected: the influence of the extraordinary complexity of Eastern verse-patterns on early mediæval song. The delight in pattern for its own sake is characteristic of Eastern art, and particularly characteristic of Islamic art in its earliest development. The civilisation that gave us the arabesque, the damascened blade and the Persian arts of carpet weaving and embroidery, gave also verse patterns almost devoid of any but conventional significance. It is not usual to accept any Eastern influence behind the quaint conceits of troubadour and jongleur at the present time. But if we consider the double Moorish and Provençal origin of the stories found in their romances, where the "beau rôle" is partially assigned to Saracen or Christian champion according to whether the bard is north or south of the Pyrenees, it seems impossible to deny some such influence; particularly if we remember the constant importation from the East of mimes, jongleurs, dancers and minstrels, which marked all periods of prosperity and of peace such as the middle years of the reign of Charlemagne. Variety of stanzaic form, rigorous rhyme-patterns and inter-woven refrains and "bourdons" which facilitated improvisation by their conventionality, all these which prepared the dawn of poetic revival can be traced to the three great schools of bardic singers in Southern and Northern France and in Italy. When Dante himself carries at one stroke the citadel of tradition, and re-establishes the "vulgar tongue," the spoken word, once more as the source and fount of poetic inspiration, he has ready to his hand delicate stanzaic forms which lead on to the sonnet and the ballade, and strong vigorous accentual rhythms out of which could be forged the glowing force of his great line.

The elaboration of stanzaic forms under the influence of rhyme is the general note of French and Italian verse in the years that followed Dante, and from the French forms Chaucer himself derives.

The ten-syllable line of Old French verse is said to admit of no less than sixteen variations. In effect it becomes a pattern of five stresses, on a line varying from nine to eleven syllables; the initial syllable being sometimes dropped, or extra syllables introduced at the end of a line, or before the second half of the line, at the cæsura or median pause. This pause also varies, sometimes occurring after the fourth, and sometimes after the fifth syllable. Here is exemplified the particular effect of accentual verse on the ear; it measures for us the passage of time by a regular recurrence of a stress. But if no more than a single unstressed syllable regularly and monotonously succeeds between each accent we grow weary of the dull iteration and begin to speak in "sing-song." The content of the verse deteriorates proportionately with this monotony and we are no longer arrested by significant and exquisite diversity, corresponding to each shade and pulse of thought or feeling. It is to this special character of stress-verse that it will be necessary to return again and again in speaking of English rhythms.

Between the age of Chaucer and that of Spenser a new world had come into being. Two influences warred in it: the force of classical inspiration, the return to tradition which dominated Italian architecture and which tried in many ways to reconcile the poetry of the New Age with classical rules; the force of an immense outpouring of passionate vitality inherent in a time which had but just seen the discovery of a new world, the release of learning from bondage, the wonders of the printing press and of all that was hoped from the "new learning." The very revival of classical influence was at first an inspiration, rather than a restraint, but with the growth of the first generation of "book-men" in western Europe, came the desire to force on the new singers the half-understood rules of the older prosody and of the later classical commentators; all seen through Latin rather than Greek art, with Virgil for epic, Seneca for dramatic and Ovid for lyric standard. How fierce the controversy was we can hardly judge; influenced by his friend Gabriel Harvey, Spenser tried to make quantity or duration of vowels and syllables the standard of metric pattern instead of a succession of accents at regular syllabic distances, the principle which was held to dominate prosody at the time when Spenser first wrote, and to which the name of "Numbers" was generally given.

His true poetic instinct soon overcame the scholastic pedantry of Harvey's teaching, but it is no bad exercise for those who wish to learn to hear quantity superimposed on accent in English rhythms to try and read the following lines as their author intended them to sound.

Māke thў sēlfĕ flŭttrīng wĭngs ŏf thў fāst flўīng
Thŏ͞ught, ănd flў fōrth ŭntŏ mў lŏve whēresōevĕr shē bē

SPENSER, *Iambicum Trimetrum.*

See yee the blind fold - ed pret-tie God, that featheréd Arch- er

Of lov - ers mis - er - ies which ma - keth his bloodie game.

SPENSER, *Elegiacs.*

It is plain that Spenser himself had not *felt* quantity.
He believed that it must interfere with "accent." That
is to say he confused stress and quantity without being
able to conceive of a delivery in which stress should be
so softened and smoothed that the tune of the verse
should be made by the varying duration of the vowels
or, failing those, of the syllables.

It is this inability to understand that, if quantity is
to dominate, stress must be greatly diminished in force
and the syllables set to a tune or cadence based on
duration of smooth-flowing vocal or continuant sounds,
which is at the root of the long and persistent confusion of "accent" and "quantity" which marks the
history of English prosody.

Robert Bridges has pointed out[1] that if the longs
and shorts of the verse be played on the choir organ
with the great diapason pulled out, the metric pattern
can be heard devoid of stress.

It is possible with a little practice and care to do the
same thing with the voice. Monotone very softly the
notes of the scansion on page 171 and then the notes of
the example set above without any thought of the
actual words set down; continue until the tune is

[1] "A Letter to a Musician." *Poetry and Drama*, September,
1914. Poetry Book Shop.

absolutely clear to the ear. Then monotone the words carefully to that tune as if it were a very *legato* plain-song setting without stress or bar division. Repeat the experiment, bringing the chaunt gradually a little closer to speech inflection without permitting any marked stress to glide in and you will soon begin to *hear* quantity.

Behind the rather futile metric controversy was a much more serious intention, the same which was to modify French poetry for over two hundred years: the desire to impose classic themes, classic standards, classic rules of construction, on the whole fabric of our Elizabethan literature. Both attempts were defeated by the triumphant growth of the drama, and above all by the genius of Shakespeare.

The nature of dramatic verse must differ profoundly from that of lyric or epic patterns. Failure to realise this difference is one great cause of the widely differing theories held on the subject of metrical delivery. Though the nature of dramatic form must be reserved for discussion in a later chapter, it is obvious that verse which is at certain moments to set up the illusion that we are listening to the interchange of speech between diverse characters, under the sway of differing emotions, and reflecting differing situation or circumstance, cannot be of too rigid and unbending a metric form.

In lyric poetry we have the unity of delivery which results from the fervent unity of the poet's mood. In epic or narrative verse we are required to accept the person of the poet as sole narrator; but in dramatic verse we have to follow each character, judging their speech by the only standard we possess, the standard of fidelity to life.

We can escape from this necessity by adopting a convention. Such a plastic convention as that which underlies Greek tragedy, where the lyric odes of chorus change the plane of the action and transcend our sense of realistic possibility; or again such a convention as that which Yeats has achieved by neglecting the accidents of individual characterisation as unsuited to poetic drama, and deliberately maintaining the atmosphere of lyric beauty throughout the play irrespective of strongly defined individuality. The Elizabethan chose neither method. Tragedy, comedy, drama, farce, all are blended in a form whose avowed object was the interpretation of life by mirroring nature. The genius of one man working at the supreme moment of our speech development, at a time when the "vulgar tongue" had just enshrined for our people the first great hope of intellectual liberty, in the matchless beauty of our Bible translation, solved this problem in so supreme a manner that we are never conscious it even presented itself to him. Of Shakespeare's mastery of metric form it is impossible to speak in detail in a work of this length. His blending of prose and blank verse, with the clear yet unjarring transition from one to another, at the exact instant when the actor needs a greater freedom of conversational pitch-inflection; the subtle variation by which age, rank, sex, character, mood, circumstance are all in turn masters of the simple ten syllables of his line; his unfailing rise to the height of every greatest argument; the easy flow of jest and repartee; the arrest or spring of the line as thought or passion dominate; these things stir one to a delight so passionate that one almost resents the necessity for analysis. Yet if that analysis be reverent and inspired it adds to all our delight in him a keener edge; it disposes with finality of all false standards of presentation for his plays, since to the ear first and above all they must make their appeal, if that beauty is to be

felt. It disposes too of the conception of our greatest
poet as an inspired imbecile who merely

> Warbles his native wood-notes wild.

One consideration alone would be sufficient to destroy
such a legend: the varying vocabulary of the plays.
But the mass of delicious mockery of bad verse; of
the "love" and "dove" banalities of the sonneteer,
of the euphuist's "honorificabilitudinitatibus," of the
pedant's Latinities; the capacity to reel off "the
right butter-woman's rank to market" or the "ill
numbers" of a Hamlet; the dexterity of parody and
colourable imitation in the *Midsummer Night*, or in
the Player's *Hecuba*: all these convince us with an ever
growing certainty that whether by divine sense of music
and unrivalled metric gift, or by deliberate mastery
of every resource of a subtle art, Shakespeare set himself to achieve a perfect medium of poetic speech for
the art of the actor.

In a sense he has done his work too well. He is
almost fool-proof where rhythm is concerned. Almost
but not quite. One has lived to see an elaborate change
of scene take place in the middle of the most perfectly
passionate lines in all the plays—so that Mark Antony's
repeated "I am dying, Egypt, dying," which haunts
our ear like the cadence of Roland's last horn-blast,
became a series of blurred and reiterated jerks, as the
great pulleys and weights of the scene-shifters wedged
and tugged the unfortunate gentleman into the anxious
arms of his swivelling Cleopatra.

But the effect of the whole mass of Elizabethan
dramatic writing, and not of Shakespeare alone, was to
break down the syllabic relation of accent and metre.
The ear became satisfied so long as the accent fell at
intervals which interpreted the throbbing rhythm of

the speaker's diction, indifferent to the exact number of unstressed syllables which fell trippingly from the tongue as they were uttered.

Take as an example these two passages, one from *A Midsummer Night's Dream*, among the earliest, the other from *The Tempest*, among the latest, of the whole series of the plays:

I know a bank whereon the wild thyme blows,
Where ox-lips and the nodding violet grows;
Quite over-canopied with luscious woodbine,
With sweet musk-roses, and with eglantine:
There sleeps Titania sometime of the night,
Lull'd in these flowers with dances and delight;
And there the snake throws her enamell'd skin,
Weed wide enough to wrap a fairy in:
And with the juice of this I'll streak her eyes,
And make her full of hateful fantasies.

Act II. Scene 1.

.   .   .   .

Ye elves of hills, brooks, standing lakes, and groves;
And ye that on the sands with printless foot
Do chase the ebbing Neptune, and do fly him
When he comes back; you demi-puppets that
By moonshine do the green-sour ringlets make,
Whereof the ewe not bites; and you whose pastime
Is to made midnight mushrooms, that rejoice
To hear the solemn curfew; by whose aid—
Weak masters though ye be—I have bedimm'd
The noontide sun, call'd forth the mutinous winds,
And 'twixt the green sea and the azur'd vault
Set roaring war:

Act V. Scene 1.

The first presents us with rhymed heroic verse; one of the patterns chosen for the conventionalised fairies of the *Dream*. Each line has a fairly marked median

E

pause, generally falling after the second foot. Quantity is of course perceptible in both passages, but in the first it has no influence on the metric pattern: we hear it, that is to say, as we hear sense-stress, or pitch, as a tune woven through the time-signature of the music, never really contradicting it but delicately embroidering it.

The favourite "trochaic" first foot, or inversion of the first foot, gives charming variety to lines 5 and 6. the sense-stress on "throws" gives an even more delicate music followed by the tripping syllables of "her enamell'd skin." A logical pause falls at the end of every line and there is no overlapping, most of the rhymes carrying a stress.

In the second there is a logical pause more or less midway in each line, and practically no end-pause in six out of the twelve lines. The major accents are reinforced by quantity, so that the effect of the lines is a passage-rhythm of stresses at equal distances of time without regard to syllabic numbers. The stressed syllables "foot," pastime," rejoice," make it possible to mark endings in three of the overlaps. In the fourth line, the sense-stress requires a slight pause after "demi-puppets" which enables "that" to transfer as an initial beat to the next line, without losing the sense of the line-ending. The rise and fall of the antithesis in "chase" and "fly him," gives the third line its cadence. Finally sense and phrasing end together at "war" after the third stress of the line,

sèt ròaring wàr.

The formless cut-up prose into which so much of the later Elizabethan verse degenerated bears no relation to the music of this beautiful lyric passage, as musical as any in our language; but what we are conscious of above all in hearing it, is the weaving of a spell against opposing forces. Of something that must be *held*, or the elusive elements will slip from our grasp as they do here:

> The elements
> Of which your swords are tempered, may as well
> Wound the loud winds, or with bemock'd-at stabs
> Kill the still closing waters, as diminish
> One dowle that's in my plume
>> (*Tempest*, Act III. Scene iii);

or when we watched that magic coach

> Drawn with a team of little atomies
> Athwart men's noses as they lie asleep
>> (*Romeo and Juliet*, Act I. Scene iv)

And then in an instant the delicate magic grows dangerous; fear steals in on us and we stand on the threshold of the black and forbidden arts. But the spell holds, the mighty wizard controls his elements,

> And, when I have required
> Some heavenly music,—which even now I do,—
> To work mine end upon their senses that
> This airy charm is for, I'll break my staff,
> Bury it certain fathoms in the earth,
> And deeper than did ever plummet sound
> I'll drown my book.

It matters little whether we hold this only the unconscious magic of the singer, or whether we see in it besides the supreme art of his latest cunning knowledge of his craft. We who would understand must weigh and trace and follow the wonder of that skill if we are to interpret that craft. How many actors, fully sensitive to the beauty of the "part" of Prospero, have we heard reduce that magic to halting prose! How many unfortunate children have "scanned" their love of poetry out of existence in the effort to reduce its subtleties to the jog-trot of a non-existent "rule"!

Another great force was conspiring with the necessities of dramatic delivery to set verse free from the too-exact bondage of "numbers." Music was beginning to follow its independent rhythms, without regard to alternating beats, and was still further confusing stress and quantity.

It is no accident that Milton—the great poet who more than any other set verse free of too slavish bondage to alternating stresses and first showed how the metric values could be heard unmarked through, and against, the method of sense-stress in verse-writing, —should have been a trained musician, and a genuine student of classical prosody.

See first exactly in what manner modern settings modified the metric and rhythmic structure of poetry.

Here are the words of one of the most beautiful of English songs followed by a setting as simple and exquisite as the words:

> Drìnk to me ònly with thine èyes
> And Ì will plèdge with mìne;
> Or lèave a kìss but in the cùp
> And Ì'll not loòk for wìne.
> The thìrst that from the soùl doth rìse
> Doth àsk a drìnk divìne;
> But mìght I of Jòve's nectar sùp
> Ì would not chànge for thìne.
>
> I sènt thee làte a rosy wrèath,
> Nòt so much hònouring thèe
> As gìving it a hòpe that thère
> It coùld not wìthered bè:

But thòu thereòn didst ònly brèathe
And sènt'st it bàck to mè;
Sìnce when it gròws and smèlls, I swèar,
Nòt of itsèlf but thèe.

Considered as metre this verse presents a very simple pattern. The first line begins with an inverted foot: anyone familiar with the exercise of scanning can tick off the scheme in regular stressed and unstressed syllables.

Here is, however, the true pattern of the passage considered as an example of "stress verse" according to the rules of Bridges' stress prosody:

Drìnk tŏ mĕ | ònlў | wĭth thīne èyes |

Ănd Ì | wĭll plèdge | wĭth mìne; |

Ŏr leàve | ă kìss | bŭt ĭn thĕ cùp |

Ănd Ì'll | nŏt loòk | fŏr wìne; |

Thĕ thìrst | thăt frŏm thĕ soùl | dŏth rìse

Dŏth àsk | ă drìnk | dīvìne; |

Bŭt mìght Ī | ŏf Jòve's | nĕctăr sùp |

Ì woŭld nŏt | chànge | fŏr thìne. |

or

Ì woūld | nòt chānge | fŏr thìne. |

Ì sènt thĕe | làte | ă rŏsў wrèath, |

Nòt sŏ mŭch | hònoŭrīng | thèe |

Ăs gìvĭng ĭt | ă hòpe | thăt thère |

Ĭt coùld nŏt | wìthēr'd | bè: |

Bŭt thòu | thĕreòn | dīdst òn-lў | brèathe, |

Ănd sènt'st ĭt | bàck | tŏ mè; |

Sìnce whēn | ĭt gròws | ănd smèlls, | Ī swèar,

Nòt | ŏf ītsèlf | bŭt thèe! |

Here is the notation of the ordinary musical setting.
It can be seen how this setting effaces the natural long
and short value of the syllables, so changing the "tune"
of the verse; but, more important still, the example
illustrates the musical lengthening of stressed notes.
Even in a passage of equal notes, the stressed beats
give a slight feeling of extra note‑length.   In
ordinary melodic writing the longer notes fall on the
accent-beat.   There is finally a beautiful variant of the
musical setting made by Dr. Aiken in which the notation corresponds much more closely to the true rhythmic
beat of the lines.

No. I.

Drink to me on - ly with thine eyes and
I sent thee late a ro - sy wreath, Not

I . . will pledge with mine ; . . Or leave a kiss with-
so . . much hon'-ring thee . . . As giv- ing it a

in . . the cup, And I'll not ask for wine ; . . The
hope that there it could not with- er'd be ; . . . But

thirst that from the soul doth rise Doth ask a drink di -
thou there-on didst on - ly breathe, And sent'st it back to

vine. . . But might I of Jove's nec - tar sip, I
me. . . . Since when it grows and smells I swear, not

would not change for thine. . .
of . . it - self but thee. . .

No. II.

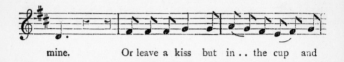

Drink to me on - ly with thine eyes and I will pledge with

mine.   Or leave a kiss but in .. the cup and

I'll not   look for wine   The thirst that from the

soul doth rise may ask   a drink di - vine, . .

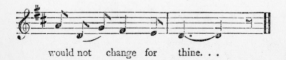

But might I   of Jove's   nec - tar sup,   I

would not   change for   thine. . .

I sent thee late a ro - sy wreath . .

Not so much hon - our-ing thee, . . As giv-ing it a

hope that there it could not with-er'd be. . . But

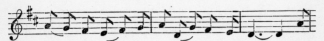

thou there-on didst on - ly breathe and sent'st it back to

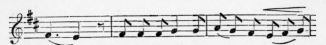

me. . . Since when it grows and smells, I swear,

not of it - self but thee. . .

During the early seventeenth century we have the age of our greatest national development in song-writing and song-setting. The later Shakespearean plays, Ben Jonson, Herrick, Heywood, the Cavalier singers; take any one of the most familiar of these lovely lyrics and say them. It is almost impossible to say the words without reproducing the rhythm of the well-known setting. Yet to one who does not know the tune such a delivery of the words will sound stilted and unpoetical. Take as an example the first line of *Cherry Ripe*:

> Cherry Ripe! Cherry Ripe! Ripe! I cry.

Who that knows the tune can give ordinary value to the five repetitions of the vowel "i" in that line, or maintain the sense-stresses of the line?

While lyric verse was being modified by the growth of musical construction, the theatre was degrading blank verse to the level of mere prose cut into lengths, a perfectly adequate vehicle for the rhetorical tricks of the actor of the day. Lyric poetry was at its most exquisite, but the theory of prosody was becoming dangerously absurd. As Mr. Omond points out in his masterly analysis of English metrists, after the defeat of the ludicrous attempts at quantitative writing already referred to, quantity and accent are involved in hopeless confusion.

Three elements must be distinguished in every spoken sound, pitch, force and duration. . . . These three elements are distinct and different, separable always in thought, separated often in practice. No analysis can be accurate which confuses them. In the books before us accent is defined sometimes as one of these (each in turn by different writers), sometimes as any two of them, occasionally as all three together.[1]

[1] *English Metrists*. T. S. Omond. Chapter II.

During this period of confusion, the greatest of English metrists, Milton, was elaborating the marvellous series of metric devices by which he

i. Maintained the nominal regularity of scansion in each line:

Of thàt | forbìd | den trèe | whose mòr | tal tàst. |

ii. Varied the actual syllabic number of his line by such devices as elision, extra metrical syllables, but never by deficiency:

Thy praises with th'innumerable sound.

. . . .

Foe not formìdable, exempt from wound, etc.

. . . .

Of Rebel Angels by whose aid aspi [ring].

iii. Varied the number of stresses in a line though their fall remains at an equal distance one from the other in point of time and is therefore named "isochronous." This is accomplished

(a) By the use of inversion:

Thèse are thy glòrious wòrks, Pàrent of gòod,
Fàirest of stàrs, làst in the tràin of nìght, etc.

(b) By actual omission of accents:

No lìght; but rather dàrkness vìsible.

The fuller study of the marvellous variety so introduced will be found in Robert Bridges' masterly analysis of Milton's prosody.[1] Sir Henry Newbolt has emphasised the fact already clearly apprehended by the Laureate, that the real effect on the ear is an exquisite balance; a compensation between the sound-pattern and the sense-pattern of the lines. The ear, expecting and recalling

[1] *Milton's Prosody, with a Chapter on Accentual Verse, and Notes,* by Robert Bridges.

the regular beat of the metric pattern, is caught and delighted by the subtle variation introduced to fit the meaning. The mind dwelling on the meaning is caught and charmed by an unexpected grace and strangeness in the fall of the stresses which we are perfectly familiar in daily speech.

And most of the beauty of the lines and all their variety is gained by the skill with which the woof of speech-rhythm is continually thrown athwart the warp of the metrical type.[1]

Before this principle, the real foundation of English verse, could be openly accepted, a long interregnum had to occur.

Two causes led to it: (1) a frank acceptance of French influence in our literature, from political and social causes; and (2) the decline of poetic inspiration in the temporary exhaustion of older forms by a freedom which led to formlessness.

French verse founded on the standard of French speech has little marked stress. So little that English ears, accustomed to the drum-beat scansion, practised in grammatical study of verse, have gone ludicrously astray on it. Recently Legouis quoted with amused bewilderment Malone's note to Dryden's *Discourse on Epic Poetry*, to the effect that the rhythm of a French Alexandrine runs exactly like

A còbbler there wàs and he lìved in a stàll.

Imagination fails at the effort so to translate the thunders of Camille's denunciation:

Rom l'ùn-ik ob-jèt |de mon rè-sen-ti-mèn |
Rom a kì |vien tong bràs |d'i-mo-lèr |mo na-màng |
A   còb | bler there wàs | and he lìv'd | in a stàll,

[1] Henry Newbolt: *A New Study of English Poetry*. Chapter II.

is probably the diction present to the English critic's mind! To French ears the rhythm of the tune is heard as a line of two sets of six equal syllables divided by a marked median pause.

By students of French diction they are first studiously practised in the most exact temporal regularity:

One two three four five six ‖ One two three four five six

Pui-se je de mes yeux ‖ y voir tomber la fou(dre)

The immediate effect of this influence on English verse was to restore the importance of regular syllabic numeration not only as a means of scansion, or measuring off of verse, but as the actual rhythmic basis of its structure. Poetry was becoming "literary," was making, that is to say, a more exact appeal to the eye, while the fine variety which the ear enjoyed, content with the temporal recurrence of stress and pause, became subject to pedantic rule.

Those of us who can remember the diction of older speakers to whom Pope and the earlier Byron, Scott and Goldsmith were the only "correct" writers can recall the inexorable syllabic measure and the drum-beat accent they imposed on such lines as:

Oh hàp-pi-nèss our bè-ing's ènd and aìm.
Good plèa-sure, eàse, con-tènt what-è'er thy nàme.
That sòme-thing stìll which pròmpts th'e-tèr-nal sìgh.
For whìch we bèar to lìve or dàre to dìe.

And realise how much underlying variety they contrived to eliminate from the lines, which we with a keener recognition both of vowel values and sense of stress would render:

Ōh hàppĭnĕss, | oūr bè-ĭng's | ènd | ănd aìm, |
Gòod | plèasūre, | eàse, | cŏntènt, | whătè'er | thy nàme, |
Thāt sòmethĭng | stìll | whĭch pròmpts | th'ĕtèrnăl sìgh, |
Fŏr whìch | wē bèar | tŏ lìve | ŏr dàre | tŏ dìe. |

The beginning of the eighteenth century marks the dawn of the age of "literature" properly so-called, the age of books; and more particularly an age of books about speech; dictionaries, manuals of "elocution," attempts at the formulation of English grammar and rhetoric: all these things brought into the art of poetry an element of scientific study, part of that great movement of inductive thought which dates from the *Novum Organum*.

Persons of poetic ability began to make their first acquaintance with poetry exclusively through books. Persons of critical ability began to search here, as elsewhere, for law. Such a natural movement tends in our age of applied science to convert every small boy into a potential engineer. The "Age of Reason" was the result of the possibility of reason about a thousand things where records were for the first time being kept and studied.

The infinitely wider knowledge of the record of speech —printing—tended to bring poetry itself under this influence; an art which should satisfy the ear, and be tested by the ear, began to be tested graphically. It is curious to realise how confused and absurd the theories evolved were, and it is interesting to find that the best and the first scientific results attained were by men like Steele (1725), Tyrwhitt (1775), and Thelwall (1812), whose concern was with speaking verse rather than with literature in its true sense. The magnificent analysis of the criticism of this period made by Mr. T. S. Omond in his *English Metrists* renders it unnecessary to trace its history more closely.

It is usual to speak as if this interruption in the main course of English metric development had been more complete and of longer duration than was actually the case. The fact that the eighteenth century was the time marked by the beginnings of serious metric study and analysis gives undue emphasis to the "correctness" of its poetry, especially because most of the theorists were much concerned with the growing study of what was called "elocution"—an artificial method of emphasising the logical and topical elements of poetry with a view to personal display rather than to poetic interpretation, and so they exaggerated and perverted natural delivery to make verse accord with these so-called rules.

In tracing the history of poetic forms in a later chapter it will be possible to show how large a measure of beautiful and spontaneous song belongs to the "Augustan" age itself, an age, be it remembered, which saw the rapid development of music to the height of its greatest achievements.

It is at the end of the century, with the work of Southey, Scott, and, above all, of Coleridge, that we find the definite acceptance of the new principle of metric structure which had always been the practical method of our greatest singers.

That principle is enshrined in the famous preface to Coleridge's *Christabel*. It was "that of counting in each line the accents and not the syllables."

> Ìs the nìght chilly and dàrk? (7)
> The nìght is chìlly but nòt dàrk. (8)

By "accented syllables" it has been presumed that Coleridge means syllables on which a sense-stress naturally falls.

It has been pointed out by Dr. Bridges and by many other metrists that he does not carry out his theory in constant practice. For example in

> Fròm her kènnel benèath the ròck (8)
> She màketh ànswer tò the clòck. (8)

he stresses "from" and "to."

But he does restore the principle which had been observed in all great Elizabethan poetry, that the ear is satisfied if the stresses recur at equal intervals of time, irrespective of whether they are divided by a regular number of syllables.

In French verse the number of syllables is the fundamental question, while the number and incidence of the very slight stresses may constantly vary.

> Tais-toi, pérfide,
> Et n'impute qu'a tói ton lâche párricide.
> Va faire chez tes Grécs admirer ta furéur:
> Va, je la désavoue, et tu me fais horréur.
> Bárbare, qu'ás-tu fáit? avec quelle fúrie
> As-tu tránché le cours d'une si belle víe?
> Avez-vous pu, crúels, l'immóler aujourd'hui,
> Sans que tóut votre sáng se soulevât pour lúi?
> Mais párle: de son sort qui t'a rendu l'árbitre?
> Pourquoi l'ássassiner? qu'á-t-il fait? a quél titre?
> Qúi te l'a dit?[1]

Andromaque, Act V. Scene iii.

The new wine of romanticism, a movement which found much of its inspiration in the awakening poetic fervour of Germany, needed new forms in which to express itself, and all poets of that wonderful group concerned themselves passionately with freedom in metrical structure. It is curious to realise that the political reaction even influenced the attitude of critics on their achievements and that the *Edinburgh Review* dogmatised on metre as vigorously as on the tenets of the French Revolution. The work of their successors, Byron, Shelley, Keats, the great lyrists, will be studied more properly in a later chapter on the history of form. In a sense the greatest poets are least dependent on ortho-

---

[1] Pointed by Kastner in his *History of French Versification* (Clarendon Press), Ch. I. page 2.

doxy or heterodoxy in poetic structure—since they themselves are the creators of both. They alone truly live
and think in the rhythm of words, and what they do is
right, no matter how we may explain it.

With the middle of the nineteenth century we come
to the first original contributions of the singers of the
new world, and it is natural enough that the greatest
of them—Walt Whitman—should begin with free verse
—that is to say with verse which discards the element
of repeated pattern. He feels only the necessity for a
temporal rhythm—a pulse-beat, passionately irregular,
unphrased by rhymed or lined construction, in which
the pointed words or syllables alone hold the pattern
together by recurrence at regular time-intervals to
which our attention is never drawn by repetition of
line-form or stanza.

This verse, and the fact that it is verse and not
prose, has been profoundly puzzling to those who see
rhythm as a recurrence of similar phenomena at regular
intervals of time. The only recurrence here is a certain
uniformity of pulse-beat which is felt by the reader
almost more than indicated by the poet. It is as if
the verse was set going to the wave-length of some
natural force, checking, changing, rising, and falling
with the life of that force. His is the most naked poetry
ever written; at its weakest the foundation of his pulse-
beat is little more than a succession of jets of breath,
sometimes prolonged to the verge of suffocation—at
others cut into gasps almost impossible to follow. At
its finest he does convey a unity with the whole emotional force of rhythm in man, and we feel his verse
almost as a natural phenomenon. At the end of his
great paragraphs a closing line crashes down like the
final chords of a cadenza, forming indeed a "refrein,"
a reining in of his tempestuous Pegasus.

F

It is not extravagant to suggest that where free verse is concerned it marks a genuine development in the racial perception of audible rhythm. Walt Whitman was a true musician and a lover of the great modern composers whose work has raised music to the level of an independent world-art.

Impatience with formal repetition and freedom of temporal structure have been growing in the work of the musician. With them freedom from logical convention, impressionism in its highest sense, has grown. Has not its influence touched all the arts and helped to render painting impatient of "subject," and pictorial reproduction, and to bring out in poetry two opposite tendencies? One, an insistence on the value of logical and emotional speech-rhythms as in themselves valid for metrical structure; the other, as in the opposite case of Swinburne, bringing the use of words and word-tunes without great regard to the logical sense they convey.

Throughout the later years of the nineteenth century phonetic study and the growth of knowledge in the æsthetic basis of all arts, had a marked influence on the work of such men as Tennyson, Browning, Rossetti and Swinburne. It was becoming clear that rhythm was a fundamental thing, that the patterns through which rhythm could express itself, whether audibly or visually, were limitless; to dogmatise on pattern when the work of a new artist might instantly annul existing theories was to court disaster. Yet it was difficult to overcome the sense that that which was being done at the moment was the only possible thing to do. The long lifework of Lord Tennyson retarded recognition of less orthodox music, and the sudden and triumphal acclamation which carried the fame of Francis Thompson to a height beyond that which his art alone could claim, marked a reaction.

To the present Laureate we owe a double debt, not only for his own exquisite verse but for a profound and serious analysis of the stress element in modern poetry. He believes that a perception of quantity is growing in English speech, and that as it does so, it will reassert itself as a principle, not as an accident, in English metre. He maintains that no stress is admissible as a pulse-beat in a line which is not at the same time a stress in the logical sense of the words which form the line. If one may venture a criticism it is that he looks to quantity to establish the durational value of a line and does not sufficiently make it clear that the stresses themselves must stand in temporal succession to each other if they are to be rhythmic, since it is only in time that we can hear or feel verse-pattern.

The Georgians are experimenting with a versatility and resource which is unbounded in all forms of lighter verse, and one or two among them are showing a technique in the true sense which marks a great step forward in the synthesis of structural theory.

I cannot close this chapter without a word of renewed acknowledgment to Mr. Omond for his masterly survey of the history of English prosody.[1] The book appeared when a large part of my own notes were already completed, and necessitated a revision of all that I had written and the reading of many of the works cited in his magnificent bibliography. I almost felt inclined to omit the present chapter in view of his immeasurably superior achievement, but it may be useful as providing a discussion of certain general elements, and all who are interested as students will infallibly pass on to his work.

[1] *Op. cit.*, *cf.* page 61.

CHAPTER IV

THE HISTORY OF POETIC FORM

FROM the very nature of its medium—speech—poetry interprets life more completely than any other art. In the range of its subjects, in the variety of its forms, in the closeness of its relationship to imagination, thought, emotion and reason, it touches the life of the race and of the individual more closely, more universally than any other art. To trace its history is to trace the racial history of humanity. At first inseparable from primitive music, it constitutes the unconscious mould and record of human thought and of the first dawn of civilisation. War song and ballad, occupational lilt or croon, song of love, courtship and marriage, the mighty impress left on the mind of the race by the passage and conflict of the seasons, the warfare of sun and darkness, of birth and death; cradle song and lament, harvest and vintage, ritual chaunt and tune, spell and oracle, all these and a hundred more of the primitive activities of the human mind we know only through some obscure folk-song, some fragment of the *Works and Days*, some nursery rhyme or proverb. There is a temptation to-day to exaggerate the compelling power of such primitive origins, to see in them not kindred experience, but hereditary preconception in which

> One race treads as another trod
> > (SWINBURNE, *Atalanta*).

We need the sharp reminder of the artist that in all the theories of the scientific historian, in all the laws and rules of the grammarian, we are never any nearer creative art; that though the nightingale sang

> To the sad heart of Ruth, when, sick for home,
> She stood in tears amid the alien corn
>
> (KEATS, *Ode to a Nightingale*),

yet the world waited through the centuries for the music of Keats, and no knowledge of the past ever enabled the critic to forecast what form the next great singer would give to his song.

Yet this knowledge of the history of poetic form is of inestimable value to us, for in a measure each child repeats the history of the race and chooses for itself, if it may choose, the poetry suited to its form of existence and to its stage in mental growth. To the neglect of such teaching is due our failure to keep in the life of the nation the vital force of poetry, a force which gives to thought, greatness, sublimity, harmony, significance and inspiration.

The complete history of poetry would be a work of many volumes. Some knowledge of its course might well take the place of the tedious details of personal biography, and the wearisome discussions of critical and linguistic problems, which absorb so much of the limited time available for the study of the mother tongue, but here it is only possible to consider what is the true relation of poetic form to the speaking of poetry, and how it may strengthen in us the capacity for appreciation and expression.

By common consent the first and greatest of all forms is that to which we give the name of Epic Poetry. It is the greatest because its very existence depends, more than any other, on grandeur, intensity and continuity of poetic inspiration. The theme of the epic is common to many lesser forms—to the ballad sequence, to narrative, or even in some instances to what is called didactic verse; to the heroic romance in which Malory enshrined our own great epic legend: but in that small number of poems which have achieved success in this mode, all these things are transfused in the light of a sustained poetic inspiration which we recognise as the greatest creative effort of which the human imagination is capable.

A twofold origin distinguished this majestic form. First we have the racial or national epic, the heroic saga. Its origins lie in the history and life of a primitive people. It requires for its creation, growth and preservation the presence of little less than a national inspiration, finding its expression in a special caste of sacred bards or singers. The final form of its record tends, as Professor Mackail has pointed out, to come into being at an age when the social state pictured in it is definitely passing into history; at the end of a feudal or heroic age. The work of Homer, or of that school of bards who wrought under his name, is the supreme instance of such an epic. It is impossible to estimate the force of its achievement. Heroic tradition, human sympathy, historic reality, all these are behind the inspiration, but of that inspiration itself we can say no more than the first singer did, when he called down the Muse herself to sing through his lips the tale of great Achilles' wrath.

This is the form of poetry which from its largeness, its simplicity, and its primitive appeal has acted most perfectly as a source of secondary inspiration to later singers. We must never cease insisting on the fact that art derives from life itself and not from pre-existing art. Yet who can measure the force of Homeric tradition, from the imitation of Virgil to the innumerable translations, versions, expansions of modern literature, from the origins of classic drama to the sonnets of Keats or of Arnold?

Elsewhere, as in Dante and in Milton, we have the deliberate selection of this, the greatest of all poetic forms, as the only one adequate to their theme, in Milton's words, to

> Justify the ways of God to Man
>
> (*Paradise Lost*).

Here poetic and religious inspiration are indistinguishable, and here again we see poetry as part of that divine revelation which incarnates for man an ideal beyond his own conceiving.

> Here vigour fail'd the towering fantasy;
> But yet the will roll'd onward, like a wheel
> In even motion, by the love impell'd
> That moves the sun in Heaven and all the stars.
>
> DANTE, *Il Paradiso*, Carey's Trans.

It may be well to remember that, except in the work of a few of the more modern epic poets, the whole of this marvellous achievement was an achievement of the spoken word. What resources can have been at the disposal of those rhapsodists to whose tenacious memory the early tradition of such poetry was entrusted we do not know. That they constantly used a slight musical accompaniment to relieve the effort of so long a recitation, to help them to overcome the intrusive conversational inflections which so readily destroy the sublimity of heroic speech, that they held their work sacred, that their persons were respected even in the most barbarous times, that even up to our chivalric age they were themselves makers as well as speakers of their great lays, this we know. It is at least arguable that the development of the visible record—of what we call literature in the narrow sense—has made such forms of poetry in the future impossible; for the existence of the written record permits a relaxation in the continuous intensity required for epic inspiration, which tends to transform it into mere narrative poetry, full of side issues, of analysis, of logical continuity, giving us a new and very wonderful form of reflective and even dramatic verse, but denying us that soaring sustained flight by which alone the speaker could enchain his audience.

It may then be asked: What has epic poetry to do with the art of verse-speaking to-day? The race of bards is extinct and the civilisation of which they formed an integral part could not be revived; if a modern epic were created it would be for readers not for hearers, a fact which in itself has sufficed to reduce modern efforts at epic writing to the level rather of didactic or narrative poetry.

The history of poetry is measured not in years, not even in centuries, but in the succession of ages since

> Old Mæonides the blind
> Said it three thousand years ago
> (FLECKER, *To a Poet a Thousand Years Hence*).

To prophesy of its future is as futile as to prophesy of the future of the race. One figure at least might even now inspire an epic: that man unsung on whose labour and endurance the fabric of civilisation has been established. The deluge which has swept away the artificial civilisation of Eastern Europe, may not inconceivably have laid bare the soil in which it will root itself. But even if no other singer of this great art should arise, the works we possess will but gain in their value to humanity. They will remain as evidence of the true place of poetry in national life, and as a

fount of undying inspiration to those who come after
us. Think for a moment of the place filled by the
Homeric legends in our own literature:

> Much have I travell'd in the realms of gold,
> And many goodly states and kingdoms seen;
> Round many western islands have I been
> Which bards in fealty to Apollo hold.
>
> Oft of one wide expanse had I been told
> That deep-brow'd Homer ruled as his demesne:
> Yet did I never breathe its pure serene
> Till I heard Chapman speak out loud and bold:
>
> —Then felt I like some watcher of the skies
> When a new planet swims into his ken;
> Or like stout Cortez, when with eagle eyes
>
> He stared at the Pacific—and all his men
> Look'd at each other with a wild surmise—
> Silent, upon a peak in Darien.
>
> KEATS, *On first looking into Chapman's " Homer."*

> As one that for a weary space has lain
> Lull'd by the song of Circe and her wine
> In gardens near the pale of Proserpine,
> Where that Æææan isle forgets the main,
> And only the low lutes of love complain,
> And only shadows of wan lovers pine—
> As such an one were glad to know the brine
> Salt on his lips, and the large air again—
> So gladly from the songs of modern speech
> Men turn, and see the stars, and feel the free
> Shrill wind beyond the close of heavy flowers,
> And through the music of the languid hours
> They hear like Ocean on a western beach
> The surge and thunder of the Odyssey.
>
> ANDREW LANG, *The Odyssey.*

Remember how our Shakespeare sang:

> In such a night as this,
> When the sweet wind did gently kiss the trees,
> And they did make no noise,—in such a night
> Troilus methinks mounted the Trojan walls,
> And sigh'd his soul toward the Grecian tents,
> Where Cressid lay that night.
>> In such a night
> Did Thisbe fearfully o'ertrip the dew,
> And saw the lion's shadow ere himself,
> And ran dismay'd away.
>> In such a night
> Stood Dido with a willow in her hand
> Upon the wild sea-banks, and wav'd her love
> To come again to Carthage
>> (*Merchant of Venice*, Act V. Scene i);

and how Hermia vowed by

> That fire which burn'd the Carthage queen,
> When the false Trojan under sail was seen
>> (*Midsummer Night's Dream*, Act I. Scene i),

or Portia visioned

> the Dardanian wives,
> With blearèd visages, come forth to view
> The issue of th' exploit
>> (*Merchant of Venice*, Act III. Scene ii),

seeing rather that last fight when Hector fell before the Scæan Gate, as Chapman sang it, than the legendary feats of young Alcides,

> When he did redeem
> The virgin tribute paid by howling Troy
> To the sea-monster
>> (*Merchant of Venice*, Act III. Scene ii).

Nor must it be forgotten that it is these great epics which have given poetry perhaps its supreme influence on the social and religious history of the race.

Homer was the Bible of the Greeks, and the revelation it conveyed to them was that of beauty expressed in things moral, physical and intellectual. Penetrating the whole consciousness of the Hellenic race, it gave to the world the earliest conscious revelation of æsthetic inspiration, as certainly as the Hebrew gave the revelation of spiritual life.

The inspiration was shortlived in its very intensity, but again and again humanity has turned back to the Greek for its teachings.

On the lips of Virgil the same inspiration passed through the splendours of the Latin tongue from the old civilisation to the new, tingeing the profoundest consciousness of religious life, and giving form even to the eschatology of the Church.

In the chivalric lays, the *Chanson de Roland*, the Arthurian legends, even in the great romances, the code and temper of chivalry impressed themselves on the modern world. Spenser found in them the dawn song of Elizabethan poetry.

The Miltonic study of human origins modified the religious consciousness of the English people, and much of its colossal imagery has taken the place of older religious teaching for thousands who have never read a line of either *Paradise*.

It was Virgil's hand led Dante from that

> mezzo del cammin
> > (DANTE, *Inferno*, Canto i),

on his tremendous round through Hell and Purgatory to the gates of the Earthly Paradise.

Arthur, in the figure of that "Magnanimity" without which

> Man is a Busie, Mischievous, Wretched Thing; no better than a Kinde of Vermine
> > (FRANCIS BACON, *Of Goodness and Goodness of Nature*),

overtops the stature of all in the *Faerie Queene* and seems
to come again from "the Island Valley of Avillion"—
whenever the tide of English song runs strongest.

> Evening on the olden, the golden sea of Wales,
> When the first star shivers and the last wave pales;
> O evening dreams!
> There's a house that Britons walked in, long ago,
> Where now the springs of ocean fall and flow,
> And the dead robed in red and sea-lilies overhead
> Sway when the long winds blow.
>
> FLECKER, *The Dying Patriot.*

A large and possibly growing proportion will know
the origin of these things only through translations, as
Shakespeare and Keats knew them; but are they to
know them as creative masterpieces, or as the source
of that most dismal of all intellectual exercises, the
"Note on a classical allusion," from which the poetically-
minded fly as from a sawdust sandwich? There is,
perhaps, no better way of making children familiar with
the true range of epic poetry than that of giving them
short, well-made sketches of the narrative and reading
to them, as perfectly as possible, long passages from
fine translations which will awaken their determination
to know the whole poem. So far the great prose translations, read with rhythmic swing, most completely
meet the demands of the case. Then let them use the
poems as the people among whom they were made
used them, as a vehicle for dramatic expression. Let
them mime the parting of Hector and Andromache or
set the quarrel of the Chiefs to their own rhymes, even
if they be as rude as those which kept alive the memory
of the "Seven Worthies" for Costard and Holofernes.
Many scenes, like the story of Nausicaa, will almost
turn themselves into plays in any wooded garden, and
if the actors may think out their dialogue from the

familiar prose translation, the elder children will have little difficulty in swinging it back into a reasonable metric form.   So poetry will mean to them from the first something greater than the sugar-sweet personal effusions of magazine verse, the conning of holiday tasks or local examination selections, or those most terrible "dramatic poems" with which the programmes of school entertainments are still occasionally made hilarious.

The great age of Greek lyric poetry follows that of the epic.   There is no question that it is in the various kinds of lyric verse that the poet most completely expresses the personal passion and individual music of his soul.

It is only necessary to remember that of the great singers of Greece nearly every one gave his name to an individual stanza or line which first served him as a personal rhythm, and afterwards was recognised and adopted as the characteristic pattern of a form of verse suited to some special emotional expression:

Mimnermus	(*circa*	600	B.C.)
Alcæus	(,,	640	B.C.)
Sappho	(,,	620	B.C.)
Anacreon	(,,	630	B.C.)
Theocritus	(,,	270	B.C.)

—each name has become associated with a measure so definite that the very thought of elegy, Alcaic, Sapphic, Anacreontic, idyll or eclogue remains bound up with the singer's individuality.

We know little of what this music really was.   The dialectical difficulties of the writing have rejoiced the heart of the grammarian, the attempts made to translate the elaborate quantitative patterns into accentual patterns—chaunt into drum-beat—without mastery of the laws of sound, or of the temporal duration of the metric units, has probably left no nearer approximation to the original music of the lines than the amusing travesty of the French Alexandrine quoted on page 62.

Yet something has survived. Some sense of the wedding of form and content in a supreme artistry which has proved at least an inspiration to modern singers, an individuality which informs the personal note of all lyric verse.

Round one name linger the most exquisite of such associations: Sappho, The Poetess, the Nightingale, pre-eminent "as the Lesbian Singer above those of other lands." Here is Swinburne's version of one of her favourite metres, the Sapphic stanza, to illustrate the inherent musical form inseparable from lyric poetry:

> Ah the singing, ah the delight, the passion!
> All the Lovers wept, listening; sick with anguish
> Stood the crowned nine Muses about Apollo;
> Fear was upon them

> While the tenth sang wonderful things they knew not.
> Ah, the tenth, the Lesbian! the nine were silent,
> None endured the sound of her song for weeping;
> Laurel by laurel

> Faded all their crowns; but about her forehead
> Shone a light of fire as a crown for ever.

> ALGERNON CHARLES SWINBURNE, *Sapphics.*

Here, taken from Professor Mackail's translation, are six among the tiny fragments by which we know her:

(*a*) Now I will sing to my fellow-women delightful things.

(*b*) My joy in the light of the sun holding within it all things radiant and fair.

(*c*) Surely I am not one of those who bear malice in their temper, but my heart is innocent.

(d) What country girl is this that bewitches your sense, one that does not know how to draw her skirts about her ankles?

(e) Death is evil; for the Gods have so judged; else they would have died.

(f) Sometime thou shalt lie dead, and no memory of thee shall be either then or afterward, for thou hast no part in roses from Pieria; but even in the chambers of Death thou shalt pass unknown, flitting forth among the dim ghosts.

J. W. MACKAIL, *Lectures on Greek Poetry*.

Here is a phonetic transcription of the famous lines to Aphrodite:

poikilóthron aιthánat aphródiιta,

pâi díos dolóploka, líssomái se;

mέι m ásaιisi mειd oníaιisi dámna,

pótnia thŷιmon,

allá tψíιd élth, ái pota kaιtérotta
tâιs émaιs áudɔιs aíoisa pέιlψi
éklyes, pátros dé dómon lípoisa
khrýισion êιlthes

árm ypazdéuksaisa, kálɔι dé s âιgon
ɔ́ιkee strúιthɔι protí gâιn mélainan
pýkna dínnente ptér ap orránɔ_áithe-
-ros diá méssɔι,

âιpsa d eksíkonto; sý d, ɔ̀ι mákaira
meidiáιsais aιthanátɔιi prosɔ́ιpɔιi
έιre ótti dêute pépontha, kɔ́ιtti
dêute kálειmi,

kóitt émɔii málista thélɔi génesthai
mainólaı thýımɔii; " tína dêute péithɔı
kái s ágɛin es ғán philótaıta? tís t, ɔ̂i
psápph, adikɛ́ei?

" kái gár ai phéugei, takhéɔis diɔ́iksei,
ai dé dɔ̂ira mɛ́i déket, allá dɔ́isei,
ai dé mɛ́i phílɛii, takhéɔis philɛ́isei
kɔuk ethéloisa"?

élthe moi kái nŷın, khalépaın dé lŷıson
ek merímnaın, óssa dé moi télessai
thŷımos immɛ́rrɛi, téleson, sý d áutaı
sýmmakhos ésso.

Swinburne's version of the equally famous fragment
to Atthis is memorable:

> "I loved thee"—hark, one tenderer note than all—
> "Atthis, of old time once"—one low long fall
> Sighing—one long low lovely loveless call
> Dying—one pause in song so flamelike fast—
> "Atthis, long since in old time overpast"—
> One soft first pause and last.
>
> ALGERNON CHARLES SWINBURNE, *Sapphics*.

Here are lines to her daughter on her deathbed:

> It is not right that there be mourning in the house
> Of Poetry; this befits not us.
> J. W. MACKAIL.

The variation of musical phrase—what is called
stanzaic form—that is to say lines which do not keep
an even length of structure but are grouped into short
series attaining or passing a climax, and drawn together,
or reined in, by a final phrase like the close of a perfect
cadence in music; a line in which the wave-lengths

form an interwoven pattern among themselves; a deliberate over-riding of the phrases and inflections of everyday speech; it is from these the lyric has derived its unlimited range and its capacity for transcending the logical significance of language.

The structural nature of Greek verse was sufficient to attain this variety without losing the sense of pattern; for time is the true foundation of audible rhythm and the structure of Greek verse was temporal, *i.e.* marked by the duration of the different syllables. Every syllable marked the passage of time, and Latin values were conventionally adjusted to the same result.

Throughout this age we perceive also that peculiar beauty which gives to lyric poetry its name and its value; that musical enriching, as it were, of the word-texture from which the poem is woven.

Beginning first in simple felicities of phrase, as perfect when they are greatly inspired as any achieved by a more formal art, they passed through a rather conscious onomatopœia to a perfection of word-music which eludes analysis.

The restoration of this quality to European verse in the modern world seems to spring from three sources:

i. In the rude barbaric chaunts where accent predominated, and lilt and swing were the effects to be aimed at, alliteration came like the beat of a big drum across the tramping feet to give the sense of accentual pattern.

> An unwinsome wood,
> Water stood under it.
> > BEOWULF.

More delicately the Kelt used assonance to mark the length of the key syllables in his lines.

ii. Late Latin, with pronunciation corrupted and

G

vowel quantity lost, found a childish pleasure in rhyme.

iii. In France these influences met the embroidery of Arabian "Maouchah," and the flowing Provençal tongue with its lack of accent, and the rhyme-richness of its inflectional structure, gave us the fanciful prosody of the troubadours.[1]

Dante in his *Vita Nuova* expressed in a similar manner the genius of Italian song. Rhyme became a fundamental principle of modern European verse:

> Rime, l'unique harmonie
> Du vers, qui, sans les accents
> Frémissants
> Serait muet au génie. T. de Banville.

In English verse it has never attained an equal degree of authority. Flecker expresses the English sense of rhyme much more perfectly:

> When from the clock's last chime to the next chime
> Silence beats his drum,
> And Space with gaunt grey eyes and her brother Time
> Wheeling and whispering come,
> She with the mould of form and he with the loom of rhyme.

Banville claimed that in French feeling for rhyme and feeling for poetry are indistinguishable. The whole character of French drama has been modified by this essential national characteristic, due unquestionably to the evenly-stressed syllables grouping themselves to a close on which a rest is made; the point where the rhyme falls. Mr. de Selincourt has pointed out how strongly Chaucer was influenced by French feeling and French laws in this respect. See also page 45.

But accent attained so great a mastery over our tongue that it relegated rhyme into a place of secondary importance in English poetry.

[1] *Cf.* page 45.

Shakespeare's use of it in dramatic verse will be described further on. Milton, under the inspiration of a reviving scholarship, denounced its jingling sound as trivial and of no true musical delight, but he gave us in his lyrics the finest examples of its use in English considered as craftsmanship.

Sabrina fair,
Listen where thou art sitting
Under the glassy, cool, translucent wave,
In twisted braids of lilies knitting
The loose train of thy amber-drooping hair;
Listen for dear honour's sake,
Goddess of the silver lake,
　　Listen and save.

Listen and appear to us
In name of great Oceanus,
By th'earth-shaking Neptune's mace,
And Tethys' grave majestic pace,
By hoary Nereus' wrinkled look,
And the Carpathian wizard's hook,
By scaly Triton's winding shell,
And old soothsaying Glaucus' spell,
By Leucothea's lovely hands,
And her son that rules the strands,
By Thetis' tinsel-slipper'd feet,
And the songs of Sirens sweet,
By dead Parthenope's dear tomb,
And fair Ligea's golden comb,
Wherewith she sits on diamond rocks,
Sleeking her soft alluring locks,
By all the nymphs that nightly dance
Upon thy streams with wily glance,
Rise, rise, and heave thy rosy head
From thy coral-paven bed,
And bridle in thy headlong wave,
Till thou our summons answer'd have.
　　Listen and save.　　　　　　*Comus.*

The texture of such poetry as this gives us something wrought of music, words so coloured with beauty and significance that they seem hardly to belong to human speech.

One thinks of the texture-painting of Velasquez or Franz Hals, of that subtle richness in colour and decoration which marked the decorative arts of the seventeenth century. Art has become more deliberate without ceasing to be spontaneous. Poetry is to be savoured by the inward ear, read from a book with leisure to try the turn of every phrase.

Song and lyric are no longer identical: the music of the lyric is complete within itself, no longer needing melodic emphasis where all is melodic, and though Milton's musicianship has much to do with the wonder of his achievement, music in Italy and France is already soaring above the level of the speaking voice and demanding only syllables which can be vocalised as a medium for its cadences.

Three divisions of lyric poetry will, in the main, present themselves to the speaker of English verse:

> The Song,
> The Sonnet,
> The Ode.

The first begins by presupposing the existence of a musical accompaniment or a melodic transcription: it is "written to an air" or composed as "lines for music." The most beautiful of the Elizabethan lyrics probably belong to the first class, and it seems not impossible that to this they owe their extraordinary singableness, —for music is very impatient of regular alternate stress, and where the poet has a tune in his mind he will fit delicate little groups of changing stresses to the musical pattern with more exactitude than when he works only in his own medium. Take as an example the 4th, 10th, 11th, and 12th lines of *O Mistress Mine*. The tune is in Queen Elizabeth's Virginal-book and was printed as early as 1599, two years before the first recorded performance of the play.

> O mistress mine, where are you roaming?
> O, stay and hear; your true-love's coming,
>   That can sing both high and low:
> Trip no further, pretty sweeting;
> Journeys end in lovers' meeting,
>   Every wise man's son doth know.
>
> What is love? 'tis not hereafter;
> Present mirth hath present laughter;
>   What's to come is still unsure:
> In delay there lies no plenty;
> Then come kiss me, sweet-and-twenty,
>   Youth's a stuff will not endure.

It is interesting to notice that such songs lend themselves to other musical settings with the greatest ease. Looked at attentively they provide very simple emotional contrasts, vowel successions which are very easy to vocalise, and show an absence of logical involution or inversion of syntax. On the other hand they accept purely metrical stresses, *i.e.* stresses not logically belonging to the sentence:

> *In* delay there lies no plenty;
> *Then* come kiss me, sweet-and-twenty.

See also Chapter III.

In a different direction the short song has proved irresistibly attractive to poets in a form which hardly seems to expect or require song for its interpretation.

An example may be given in the exquisite dirge from *Cymbeline*:

> Fear no more the heat o' the sun,
>   Nor the furious winter's rages;
> Thou thy worldly task hast done,
>   Home art gone, and ta'en thy wages:
> Golden lads and girls all must.
> As chimney-sweepers, come to dust.
>
> Fear no more the frown o' the great;
>   Thou art past the tyrant's stroke;
> Care no more to clothe and eat;
>   To thee the reed is as the oak:
> The sceptre, learning, physic, must
> All follow this, and come to dust.
>
> Fear no more the lightning-flash,
>   Nor th' all-dreaded thunder-stone;
> Fear not slander, censure rash;
>   Thou hast finish'd joy and moan:
> All lovers young, all lovers must
> Consign to thee, and come to dust.
>
> No exorciser harm thee!
> Nor no witchcraft charm thee!
> Ghost unlaid forbear thee!
> Nothing ill come near thee!
> Quiet consummation have;
> And renowned be thy grave!
>
> Act IV. Scene ii.

Considering the great amount of such poetry it is inevitable that much of it should sink far below the level of that excellence which lyric poetry demands. Owing to its formal character no other range of poems so quickly becomes conventional, derivative and false. It is perhaps more extraordinary that there should be so much that is excellent in verse which seems

so temptingly easy as this. These short song-lyrics,
dramatic lyrics, "verses," number the best as well as
the worst of modern poetry.

> Herrick's and Wordsworth's *Daffodils*,
> Shelley's lines *To Night*,
> Browning's *O, to be in England*,
> Tennyson's songs in the *Princess*,
> Yeats' *Innisfree*,
> Flecker's *In Phæacia*,
> Thomson's *Last Lines*,
> Ralph Hodgson's *Miracle*,
> Alice Meynell's *Shepherdess*,

are examples that rise instantly to one's thoughts.

If we expand the definition of the form a little more
widely in the direction of the ballad and of narrative
or didactic poems, we find here a golden thread of
poetry which held through times when all other inspiration seemed broken. The later eighteenth century gave
us Burns, Lady Nairne, Scott and the hymns of Addison,
Cowper, Watts and Wesley, and it was through the
ballad itself that English poetry was re-born at the
beginning of the nineteenth century, and Dobell's
Keith of Ravelstone or Keats' *Belle Dame sans Merci*
prove that the purely lyric elements of the ballad
are sufficient to give it rank in the greatest tradition
of English poetry.

This is the type of verse which is most often spoken
or read aloud, and which perhaps gains most in the
speaking; for it is full of personal emotion which is
yet sufficiently set out and stabilised to be rendered
with some measure of tranquillity. It is the line of
most direct appeal to a public which can endure being
sung to but not being spoken at.

Nowhere is sense of style a more absolute necessity

than in dealing with work of this kind. The effects at which such poems aim are lyric, never dramatic. It is the music of the verse, poetic richness in the texture of the poem, concentration and avoidance of all didactic, argumentative, or explanatory inflections which must be felt. These words of Professor Mackail give the best guide to the danger which besets the speaker as closely as the poet:

The lyric follows instinct; and in the immense range and difference of instinct lies the range of lyric poetry, and the difference—the greatest of all differences in poetry —between the good lyric and the bad. There is another difference almost as great; that between the true lyric and the false. This does not lie in a difference of emotional instinct, but in the difference between a real emotion and one which is secondary, induced, or simulated.

Two things the poet himself warns us to avoid—any gesture, except possibly that which inevitably follows from our personal absorption in the beauty of what we speak; and elaborate voice-inflection reducing the poetry of the lines to chatty or argumentative tones. Picture the opening verse of Keats' poem so delivered, and refrain!

> O what can ail thee, knight-at-arms,
>   Alone and palely loitering?
> The sedge has wither'd from the lake,
>   And no birds sing.

The second form, that of the sonnet, presents the finest medium for the study of the history and achievement of modern lyric poetry, for in it are reflected the faults and excellences of every period.

Derived from the group of artificial verse-forms of the Italian "Lingua di Sì" [1] early in the 13th century, it

---

[1] Pier delle Vigne, Secretary of State to the King of Sicily about 1220, is the first known writer of the sonnet.

owes something, particularly in its closing lines, to the Greek epigram and elegy. It has alone survived as a fully expressive poetic form from the age which gave us the numberless patterns of the rondeau, villanelle, chant royal, ballade and triolet. That is to say all these are still written, but, with the possible exception of the ballade, they are written as exercises in form, not as expressive art; the sonnet lives. It may not be superfluous to analyse its form: It is of the ordinary three - quatrain length, with an added two lines, of which the last should sum up the whole thought of the poem in the manner of the Greek elegiac epigram:

> Not my namesake of Chios, but I, who belong
> To the Syracuse burghers, have sung you my song.
> I'm Praxagoras' son by Philinna the fair,
> And I never asked praise that was owing elsewhere.
>
> CALVERLEY, *Theocritus : Epigrams and Epitaphs.*

The rhymes of the fourteen lines are interwoven so as to help the continuity of the poem; the most approved order being abba, abba, cde, cde, or cd, cd, cd. But the true division of the poem should be into two groups of eight and of six lines, the octave and the sestet, one stating and the other answering a continuous train of thought in the poet's mind:

> Mysterious Night! when our first parent knew
> Thee from report divine, and heard thy name,
> Did he not tremble for this lovely Frame,
> This glorious canopy of Light and Blue?
>
> Yet 'neath a curtain of translucent dew,
> Bathed in the rays of the great setting Flame,
> Hesperus with the Host of Heaven came,
> And lo! Creation widen'd on man's view.

> Who could have thought such Darkness lay concealed
> Within thy beams, O Sun! or who could find,
> Whil'st flower, and leaf, and insect stood revealed,
> That to such countless orbs thou mad'st us blind!
>
> Why do we then shun Death with anxious strife?
> If Light can thus deceive, wherefore not Life?
> J. BLANCO WHITE, Night and Death.

The hardness of its craftsmanship gives to the sonnet something of the quality of a cameo or carved gem, and as in these, we can endure in it the treatment of the greatest and most sublime subject without the sense that it exceeds the measure of so small a space.

But the range of the sonnet is its most astounding characteristic. After reading the two volumes of Sir Sidney Lee's *Elizabethan Sonnets* we feel that no possible variant of so strict a form can have been left untried by the writers. Yet even these derive from their great master Petrarch (1304–74):

> Methought I saw the grave where Laura lay,
> Within that temple where the vestal flame
> Was wont to burn; and passing by that way
> To see that buried dust of living fame,
> Whose tomb fair Love and fairer Virtue kept,
> All suddenly I saw the Fairy Queen;
> At whose approach the soul of Petrarch wept;
> And from thenceforth those Graces were not seen,
> For they this Queen attended; in whose stead
> Oblivion laid him down in Laura's hearse.
> RALEIGH, Lines on the Faery Queene.

The mood of impatience with the formal sonneteer was familiar to Shakespeare who mocked:

> Tush, none but minstrels like of sonneting.
> Love's Labour's Lost.

Yet

> With this same key
> Shakespeare unlocked his heart! once more!
> Did Shakespeare? If so, the less Shakespeare he!
>
> ROBERT BROWNING, *House*.

It is difficult, indeed, for a belief in the personal passion of the Shakespearean sonnets to survive any prolonged study of this mass-production during Elizabethan days.

Rather do we see a momentary desire to escape into personal utterance, to accomplish the perfection of a "fine filed" phrase, without the disturbing consciousness of a player's personality between him and his hearers, and surely, at times, a conviction beyond words and beyond doubt of the immortality of his own fame.

> If this be error and upon me proved,
> I never writ, nor no man ever loved.
>
> SHAKESPEARE, *Sonnets*, No. 116.

Shakespeare chose the easier form of three quatrains and a couplet, and holds us suspended in wonder and delight while again and yet again the magic works, and words, and thought, fire - new, fall into their appointed beauty.

> No longer mourne for me when I am dead
> Than you shall hear the surly sullen bell
> Give warning to the world that I am fled
> From this vile world, with vilest worms to dwell;
>
> Nay, if you read this line, remember not
> The hand that writ it; for I love you so,
> That I in your sweet thoughts would be forgot
> If thinking on me then should make you woe.

O if, I say, you look upon this verse
When I perhaps compounded am with clay,
Do not so much as my poor name rehearse,
But let your love even with my life decay;

Lest the wise world should look into your moan,
And mock you with me after I am gone.

SHAKESPEARE, *Sonnets*, No. 71.

The capacity for sustained expression: for holding through the thought against the formal scheme and the often unstressed rhymes, is the first necessity for study when speaking a sonnet. Milton, Wordsworth, and above all Keats, the Women Poets, to whose facility of emotion it provided a most exquisite resistance, Matthew Arnold, Rossetti, Swinburne, Rupert Brooke: the chain of excellence is unbroken.

Lest we should grow to fancy some transcendent sympathy between our national genius alone and this form, turn for an instant to this exquisite example from the French:

Le Séraphin des soirs passe le long des fleurs . . .
La Dame-aux-Songes chante à l'orgue de l'église;
Et le ciel, où la fin du jour se subtilise,
Prolonge une agonie exquise de couleurs.

Le Séraphin des soirs passe le long des cœurs . . .
Les vierges au balcon boivent l'amour des brises;
Et sur les fleurs et sur les vierges indécises
Il neige lentement d'adorables pâleurs.

Toute rose au jardin s'incline, lente et lasse,
Et l'âme de Schumann errante par l'espace
Semble dire une peine impossible à guérir. . . .

Quelque part une enfance très douce doit mourir . . .
O mon âme, mets un signet au livre d'heures,
L'Ange va recueillir le rêve que tu pleures.

ALBERT SAMAIN (Van Bever et
Paul Léautaud, *Poètes d'Aujourd'hui*, p. 315).

The third and greatest of the lyric forms with which the speaker has to concern himself is the ode. In its Greek origins it was a dance-song either in its dramatic chorus form, in the Dionysiac ritual, or in the celebration of victory, of festival, or finally in the Pindaric odes (521–441 B.C.) as a song in honour of any individual or enterprise. It was the dancing which made clear the pattern and the musical phrasing that served to interpret the scansion of these complicated patterns. But we need turn to no ancient origins in considering this form, since in our own language we have the most perfect masterpieces which it has inspired. Milton's *On the Morning of Christ's Nativity*, Dryden's *St. Cecilia's Day*, Wordsworth's *Intimations of Immortality*, and above all Shelley's *West Wind*, Keats' *Nightingale, Grecian Urn* and *Psyche* mark the highest level of English lyric poetry.

The keynote of these beautiful poems is a certain intensity, a flinging of heart, soul, and imagination into a series of vivid pictures. In each of them we find a triple thread; a close correspondence of sound and sense, like the perfect onomatopœia of the *West Wind*; a force of visual description which creates its own atmosphere; and then the working of all this within the poet's own heart, so that the storm without transmutes itself into the force of his own passion.

> . . . . a light spear topped with a cypress cone,
> Round whose rude shaft dark ivy-tresses grew,
> Yet dripping with the forest's noonday dew,
> Vibrated, as the ever-beating heart
> Shook the weak hand that grasped it; . . . .
>
> SHELLEY, *Adonais*.

In the *West Wind*, the shortest and in some ways the most perfect of the series, we have the three pictures of the wind, in leaves, in clouds, and in the waves,

descriptively so accurate that they might have been
written by one trained in scientific observation.

> . . . . . while far below
> The sea-blooms and the oozy woods which wear
> The sapless foliage of the ocean, know
> Thy voice, and suddenly grow grey with fear,
> And tremble and despoil themselves.
>
> SHELLEY, *Ode to the West Wind*.

We can sit and visualise each verse alone as a picture
without thought of the words as if it were a memory
from Nature herself. Yet the words alone with their
rush, climax, and fall, their contrast and swiftly moving
pace, seem capable of suggesting the whole imagery
of the poem to one who was ignorant of their verbal
significance. In the last two verses the poet is one
with the wind,

> . . . . . only less free
> Than thou, O, uncontrollable!   *Ibid.*

and personal experience itself opens out into the universal; the wind becomes the breath of the quickening
spirit of life on the dead ashes of human failure.

> Scatter, as from an unextinguished hearth
> Ashes and sparks, my words among mankind!
> Be through my lips to unawakened earth
> The trumpet of a prophecy! O, wind,
> If Winter comes, can Spring be far behind?   *Ibid.*

So, at the last, in his prophetic vision of his own end
he was to invoke the same inspiration:

> The breath whose might I have invoked in song
> Descends on me; my spirit's bark is driven
> Far from the shore, far from the trembling throng
> Whose sails were never to the tempest given;
> The massy earth and sphered skies are riven!
> I am borne darkly, fearfully, afar;
> Whilst burning through the inmost veil of Heaven,

The soul of Adonais, like a star,
Beacons from the abode where the Eternal are.
SHELLEY, *Adonais*.

The two great elegies of Milton and Shelley, *Lycidas*
and *Adonais*, belong really to this class of poetry, though
they derive in their mechanical setting from the last
singers of Hellas, Moschus' lament for Bion, and that of
Thyrsis for Daphnis amid the flocks of a classic Sicily.

To speak the odes adequately is probably the most
difficult of all tasks for the reciter. They are dithyram-
bic, that is to say they mount in a succession of shorter
climaxes to one height of supreme intensity, and then
resolve again into a harmonious close. They have in them
the excitement of a dance of words; the danger of using
argumentative or admonishing voice-inflections is very
great, but monotony is equally insupportable. There is
a modern poem by Ralph Hodgson, *The Song of
Honour*, which, though it lacks the direct address of the
ode, illustrates the force and rapture of such poetry at
its best. It rises with every catalogue of song to the
most perfectly measured climax, so closely wrought into
the poem that it is almost impossible to quote from it.

The music of a lion strong
That shakes a hill a whole night long,
A hill as loud as he,
The twitter of a mouse among
Melodious greenery,
The ruby's and the rainbow's song,
The nightingale's—all three,
The song of life that wells and flows
From every leopard, lark and rose
And everything that gleams or goes
Lack-lustre in the sea.
RALPH HODGSON, *The Song of Honour*.

No work by a living singer speaks in surer tones of

the enduring inspiration of English poetry. Few poems in our language are more speakable.

It is particularly valuable to use the work of living men, for not only are we naturally most easily in sympathy with their thought, but we can obtain from themselves some judgment on the manner they would choose for its speaking. They cannot show us what they mean, for English poets are rarely trained speakers of verse; but they can tell us where we go wrong and help us to understand their intention. Besides, by having the courage to praise the work of living men, fearlessly, and at the risk of future disillusion, we help to dispel the mischievous impression that a poet must always be safely dead, and preferably starved to death, before he can claim to be that mysterious thing, a "classic."

The study of methods of dramatic verse-speaking must occupy so large a part of a later chapter that it will be sufficient here to summarise briefly the historic development of dramatic poetry. Its origin was ritual: a showing forth of the god in a form which created a synthesis of sight and hearing.

Greek drama, in which it had its European origin, was an act of worship to the vine-god Dionysus, with his temple as the theatre, his priests as the actors; dances which were the expression of the rituals of the various deities concerned in the action; music of flutes and harps which lifted the speech of the players to different planes of lyric or dramatic expression, and, holding it all together, spoken oration and dialogue which gave some measure of coherence to a familiar plot. Now one element and now another predominated, but always, in the great age of Greece, the true beauty of its appeal lay in the chorus. Probably no art form has ever been so completely elaborated and so hopelessly lost. It is not until the drama is in its decline that the great actor begins to attain fame, but the great dancer, singing, or rather chaunting as I have already indicated, under the direct rule of the metric form and leading his trained company, who for months had studied every movement and every word of their odes, stands out from the first as an almost mythical figure. To obtain leave to compete in the dramatic festival was "to be given a chorus." The charges of their training and costumes were paid by wealthy citizens as their tax to the state. Two-thirds of the space available for action in the theatre was reserved for their evolutions. The texts that remain to us, as in the case of the Japanese Noh Plays, are little more than a skeleton on which their art was built. The difficulty of recapturing this wonderful appeal to-day lies in the divorce between music and the spoken word. Chaunts inevitably tumble back into a long succession of alternate stresses, effacing the metric variety of such faultless lyrics as those for instance of *Atalanta in Calydon*, and inevitably they recall melancholy and didactic associations. But against the varied rhythms and orchestral timbres of modern music words are powerless, and no one has yet quite solved the problem of a setting which will follow the verse syllable by syllable and yet fulfil the expectations of colour and harmony which music to-day calls up in us. So the later plays of the Greek dramatic cycle, *The Trojan Women* or the *Iphigenia in Tauris*, where dramatic conditions make melody unsuitable and where very simple ritual movements are obviously required, have been, in the main, most successful; next to them perhaps comes the wonderful "Spring Song" of the *Atalanta* to Muriel Elliot's music and Bantock's truly Sophoclean setting of the *Electra*, to many of us the most Greek of all the tragedies. Here is a passage from a lament set to his musical notation:

H

X. ὦ παῖ, παῖ, δυσ-τα-νο-τά-τας Ἠ-λέκ-τρα ματ-ρός, τίν᾽ ἀ-εὶ

* C. O child child, of a mother unblest,   E - lect- ra why ev - er a-new

τάκ- εις ὧδ᾽ ἀ-κόρ-εστ-ον οἰ -μωγ - ὰν

art thou ceaselessly mourning thy fa — ther,

τὸν πάλαι ἐκ δολερ-ᾶς ἀθ-ε-ώ-τα-τα

Wick - ed - ly snared by thy false moth-ers' treach - er - y

ματ - ρὸς ἀλ-όντ᾽ ἀπ - ά-ταις Ἀ-γα-μέμ-νο-να

Das - tard - ly slain he, our King A - ga - men - non.

κα - κᾷ τε χει - ρὶ πρό - δο - τον ;

May he who wrought such a deed

ὡς ὁ τά - δε πορ- ὼν ὄλοιτ᾽, εἴ μοι θέμις τάδ᾽ αὐδᾶν.

per - ish ; such is my prayer, If sinless I may utter such a word.

ΗΛ. ὦ γε - νέθ- λα γεν - ναί - ων,

E. Daugh - ters of con - so - la - tion

* Note the English version is that used for the Scala Theatre performance in 1914.

pp

ἤ - κετ' ἐμ- ῶν καμ-άτ- ων πα - ρα - μύ - θι - ον.

Ye who have felt with me shar - ing my sol - it - ude

οἶ - δά τε καὶ ξυ-νί-η - μι τάδ', οὔ τί με

Well do I know that ye come but in love to me.

φυγ-γάν-ει· οὐδ' ἐθ-έλ-ω προ-λιπ- εῖν τό - δε,

Yet can-not I leave my task un - ac - com - plishéd

μὴ οὐ τὸν ἐμ- ὸν στενάχ-ειν πα-τέρ' ἄθ - λι-ον.

If I must cease from my strong la - men - ta - tion

ἀλλ' ὦ παντοίας φιλότητος ἀμειβόμεναι χάριν,
pp

Then, oh friends, dear friends! in kindliest, tenderest pity I

ἐᾶτέ μ' ὧδ' ἀλύειν, αἰαῖ, ἱκνοῦμαι.

Entreat you now to leave me Lonely in sorrow.

X. ἀλλ' οὔ - τοι τόν γ' ἐξ 'Αϊ - δα παγ - -

Yet from that black realm Hades rules

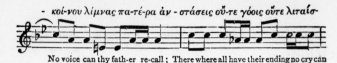

κοί-νου λίμνας πα-τέ-ρα ἀν - στάσεις οὔ-τε γόοις οὔτε λιταῖσ-

No voice can thy fath-er re-call ; There where all have their ending no cry can

- ιν.   ἀλλ' ἀ-πὸ τῶν μετρί-ων ἐπ' ἀ-μή - χανον

reach   Fa - tal the cause of thy measureless wretchedness.

ἄλ - γος ἀ - εὶ στε-νά-χου - σα δι - όλ - λυ - σαι,

Dai - ly we see cure-less sor - row des - troy-ing thee.

ἐν οἷς   ἀ - νά - λυ - σίς ἐστ - ιν

Such grief   brings no   de - li - rance   no

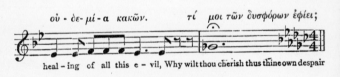

οὐ - δε-μί - α κακῶν.   τί μοι τῶν δυσφόρων ἐφίει;

heal-ing of all this e - vil, Why wilt thou cherish thus thine own despair

ΗΛ.   νήπιος ὃς τῶν οἰκτρῶς

E.   Fool - ish the child and thank - less,

οἰχ - ομ - έν - ων γον - έ - ων ἐπ - ι - λάθ - ετ - αι.

Who could for – get such a death as my fa – ther felt;

ἀλλ' ἐμ - έ γ' ἀ στον - ό - εσσ' ἄρ - αρ - εν φρένας,

Dear – er to me is that mourn – er un–wearied who

ἅ "Ιτ - υν, αἰ - ἐν "Ιτ - υν ὀλ - οφ - ύρ - ετ - αι,

"I – tys," ah, "I – tys," so sad – ly re – i – te–rates

ὄρν - ις ἀτ - υζ - ομ - έν - α Δι - ὸς ἄγ - γελ - ος.

Sor – row – ful bird that is ev – er Zeus' mes – sen – ger

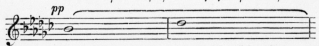

ἰὼ παντλάμων Νιόβα, σὲ δ' ἔγωγε νέμω θεόν,

pp

And so wails Mourning Niobe I at least hail her, divinest Queen,

ἅτ' ἐν τάφῳ πετραίῳ αἰεὶ δακρύεις.

In rock-hewn tomb, Lonely for ever.

From the Greek have derived, at long distance, forms of opera and ballet, and one attempt was made to do for the epic cycle of Germany what the Greek dramatists did for the stories of Agamemnon and Œdipus: Wagner's *Nibelungenlied*. If we ask ourselves why it remains a glorious and colossal failure and not as he would have it be—a new art form—the answer seems to be, first, lack of proportion in the elements of sight and sound; but above all the fact that then, as now, the true art of the theatre was not in existence; once the master stepped outside his province as a musician, he was in the position of a magnificent improvisor, trying to play an instrument of which he knew nothing; but on his creation may yet rise the music-drama of the future. For the moment two elements, music and movement alone, are being combined, with the words left out, and so we are given the kaleidoscope of Russian ballet, nearer, at its best, as we saw it when Mordken and Pavlova danced the Bacchanal, to recapturing the primal glory of Dionysiac art than any modern drama.

Of our Shakespeare and the Elizabethan drama as a whole, it is useless to speak in general terms, only remembering that its poetry primarily interprets character and circumstance, and shows, through them and through their clash, the poet's interpretation of life. While in France the accidents rather than the essentials of both give us the comedy and the keenly barbed satire which, later on, in the hands of our Restoration dramatists, were to drive all poetic form from the theatre.

Unquestionably poetry cannot sustain itself there without the strength of the most universal appeal, such an appeal for instance as Shakespeare makes in a play like *Twelfth Night*, and since the days of Ben Jonson the theatre has become only sectional: to please here is to be despised elsewhere; and so the topical element, which is the destruction of poetry, has predominated more and more; again, poets are rarely men of the theatre and so cannot write plays. Such splendid exceptions as Barker and Housman's *Prunella*, Drinkwater's *Lincoln*, or above all Hardy's *Dynasts* only serve very effectually to prove the rule. One other exception must be made—the " Little Theatre " in Abbey Street, Dublin, where Yeats and Synge found in the love of Ireland, and even in the satirising of her follies, the dayspring from on high which is needed for poetic drama. Guarding themselves fastidiously from the influences whose very strength and beauty of past accomplishment militate against the revival of dramatic poetry in England, they found an art delicate, lyric, single in its appeal, and in their varying ways did restore poetry to the stage.

To-day we are faced more and more with the sectional break-up of dramatic forms; here the pleasure of the eye alone, and here the mocking spirit of cynical satire: here magnificent realistic achievement; here jejune and precious poetic efforts; but though the cinema has ousted drama from the majority of our provincial theatres, I believe we are in view of a revival. Drama is coming again from the people themselves; and their insistent demand is for a theatre which shall get back to fundamentals; which shall re-create and interpret life for them in terms of the theatre, but with universal appeal to the truth and validity of human experience.

Perhaps the only general remark that can be made on verse-speaking in the theatre to-day is a criticism of its lack of sense of distinction. I believe nothing would help here so much as practice in those delicate satyric forms which have survived in French dramatic poems and which form the most perfect school for diction. I shall speak later of Clifford Bax's experiments in this direction.

CHAPTER V

THE ELEMENTS OF VERSE-SPEAKING

THE greater part of the elaborate directions, "rules" and "methods" devised by teachers of "elocution" to help speakers of verse, are nothing but attempts to find a substitute for true understanding and love of poetry and for natural taste and distinction in utterance.

Those who need such rules are not ready to speak verse at all; they often attain worse and more unendurable results in proportion as they are pedantic and exact in observing the rules they have been taught; as vulgar and pretentious people grow more unbearable when they affect a meticulous care for elegance.

The more persuaded we are that poetry, like all art, is the result of a direct and spontaneous inspiration of the singer, that the poet is not fettered by the thousand rules of the metrist, that these are, in fact, rather deduced from the practice of the poet than imposed on him by authority, the more certain we become that as in colour, in music, in sculpture, the laws which the poet unconsciously obeys are not the outcome of ingenious devising, or of social convention, but are fundamentally connected with the essential laws of movement and of construction.

It is only by a deeper understanding of the significance of rhythm that this synthesis can be effected.

The creative force of the poet is his perception and love of beauty. The patterns he creates conform to eternal laws which we are only beginning to perceive, laws conditioned, as in all other art, by the nature of his medium. And that medium is speech, the speech which is his mother-tongue.

It is then certain that there is no possible substitute for intelligence, significance and personal taste in the speaking of poetry; that an appreciation of content as well as form is essential; yet many scholars have been conspicuous by their inability to express a single line of verse adequately in utterance. Even the poets themselves, with rare and brilliant exceptions, are unable to convey to an audience audible significance, or any rhythm beyond a monotonous and metric scansion. Within their own minds they know their intention, but they cannot bring it out in utterance for others. What is the nature of our speech in utterance?

i. It is a musical instrument having for its source of power the breath, for its vibratory element the note, for its resonator the vowel.

ii. It is the instrument of logical expression through speech, by gradation of power, pitch or quality, by clarity, by articulation, by richness of vocabulary and by clear phrasing.

iii. It is an interpretative instrument, blending these two opposed elements in unconscious emotional or artistic expression and so gaining control and perfect transparency of expression.

The first and most important element in training utterance is the voice. In regard to what is generally called voice production it is not proposed to enter into detailed analysis or instruction in this book: not from any uncertainty in regard to method, but because it is impossible to teach these things except orally. No description, symbol or definition, no diagram or mathematical calculation will ever convey the sense of the beauty of vocal tone.

> What they could my words expressed,
> O my love, my all, my one!
> Singing helped the verses best;
> And when singing's best was done,
> To my lute I left the rest.
>
> ROBERT BROWNING.

Four factors are recognisable in the voice:

1. Breath.
2. Note.
3. Tone.
4. Vowel.

The foundation of all good voice-training lies in the management of the respiratory forces.

A clear distinction must be recognised between training intended to improve the general standard of normal respiration during all the activities of ordinary life, and that intended to meet the special requirements of the singer or speaker.

The former of these is of paramount importance, and the first principle of voice-training should be that nothing must be taught under the plea that it is necessary for the singer or speaker, which can in any way modify the natural balance and freedom of breathing in everyday life.

Ordinary breathing may be considered in these degrees:

(a) During sleep or repose,
(b) During action,
(c) During effort or violent exertion,

each passing at times into the level of the next.

(a) During sleep or repose, breathing, like all other activities, is carried on at the lowest possible

level of effort and of consciousness. All voluntary effort ceases, those muscles only which are
most nearly involuntary in their action come
into play, the requirements of the brain, heart
and lungs are reduced to their lowest point,
and no interference with this relaxed condition
can be of value to the sleeper. The ordinary
movements of waking, such as stretching and
yawning, illustrate this point very clearly; there
is an immediate demand for greater muscular
action in breathing, for a larger chest expansion,
for more air in the lungs. Breathing in repose
is carried on almost exclusively by the rise and
fall of the floor of the chest — the diaphragm;
the abdominal muscles being relaxed, the descent
of the diaphragm is accompanied by a marked
forward movement of the abdominal wall; this
is particularly noticeable in the case of a person
lying completely at rest.

(b) During action a more vigorous movement is required: the floor of the chest still descends, but
in the erect position the abdominal muscles are
no longer relaxed below the waist-line; at the
same time the muscles of the chest-wall act
with an easy, regular swing, raising the ribs and
so increasing the size of the chest-cavity in every
direction. The ribs form a cone-shaped frame
for the chest, and in free and natural breathing
the action of the muscles of the ribs gets the
largest swing just above the base of this cone,
while the descent of the floor of the chest is felt
through the forward movement of the "V"-shaped
space between the ends of the lower ribs, just
above the natural waist-line. The upper ribs
join in front to the sternum; when the whole

action of breathing is properly carried through, the sternum is slightly arched forward. This movement is promoted by the erect poise of the figure, which flattens the abdominal muscles and maintains them in a state of slight tonicity. If the abdominal muscles are drawn back during inspiration, the movement of the top of the chest becomes exaggerated and full of effort. If they are unduly relaxed, the descent of the diaphragm becomes too marked and the ribs fail to lift properly, while the sternum remains depressed as in expiration.

(c) During physical effort (i) the breath is sometimes completely held, in order to fix the chest when it is full of air. The abdominal muscles are then sharply drawn back, the shoulders a little raised, the top of the chest sharply arched forward. This breathing can be seen clearly in a diver getting ready for a long under-water swim. (ii) In strong exertion such as very long and exhausting running, the extra muscles of respiration increase the rise and fall of the sternum, and even raise the collar-bones in the effort to to get help for the heart. This breathing is never normal and can only be carried on for a short time without great distress.

It is obvious that each of these forms of breathing has a natural function to fulfil. In the normal healthy human being, each comes into play unconsciously at its proper moment, without voluntary effort on our part. The first point in respiratory training must therefore be to ensure that the individual is able to answer each demand in turn as it occurs. No amount of breathing practice in one direction will make up for lack of complete balance in the whole function of breathing. The singer or speaker must therefore work for the development of the most perfect possible poise of the figure in ordinary life, the unconscious rhythmic control which balances action and reaction, contraction and relaxation in the whole neuro-muscular system. This training is mental as well as physical, and is a vital factor in the general maintenance of health.

The voice is the first thing to show evidence of the slightest disturbance of this balance, which, like every other form of rhythmic action, consists in the exact unconscious measuring of the force required to accomplish a given movement without antagonistic action within given limits of space and time; good vocal tone is impossible without such perfect co-ordination.

We therefore ask: In what way does breathing for voice differ from normal breathing? At which of the three levels of natural respiration is it carried on? What training will establish and maintain it?

(1) The singer requires a large volume of air and particular control over it.

(2) He must be able to take in a full breath rapidly and distribute its output over a period of many seconds.

(3) Not only the output of air, but also the air-pressure in the chest during the whole period of song and speech, must be included in the control.

(4) The air-pressure in the chest and windpipe is alone responsible for the sound of the voice, and voice must always be associated with an outward movement of the breath.

(5) This outward movement of air must coincide absolutely with the instant when the sound begins; that is to say, with the drawing together of the vocal membranes.

(6) Every emphasis implies an increase of breath-pressure for a louder sound.

(7) The fundamental physical principle of the voice is the transformation of air-pressure in the chest into sonorous vibration by the "reed action" of the vocal membranes. This involves only two things:

    (a) Regulation of the breath;

    (b) Unconscious action of the vocal membranes under the direction of the ear. These must be entirely free from any tightening of the muscles about the throat, *e.g.* the muscles of the tongue, palate, jaw and lips.

The central level, that of breathing for action, is the only level at which these conditions can be fulfilled, and it is at the same time the only level it is safe to develop by direct practice: other forms, like that for repose or that for effort, fail because they exaggerate either

    (a) The abdominal action, so injuring the health, and using also the form of breathing least capable of voluntary control during expiration,

or

    (b) Upper costal action, movement of the upper ribs, which interferes with freedom of the throat muscles, and is often associated with forcible retraction of the abdominal muscles during inspiration.

It must be repeated—the question is not whether these levels of breathing have not their natural uses; rather it is whether breathing *practice* at that level can be used as a foundation for voice-training with advantage to the singer.

By the use of the central level no natural respiratory action can be interfered with, and the fullest inspiration for voice can be most rapidly accomplished.

The singer requires in the first place full use of his ribs and diaphragm in inspiration. The greatest increase in rib-expansion is obtained with the movable lower ribs and not with the rigid upper ones. On the level of about two finger-breadths below the end of the breast-bone expansion affects the widest part of the lungs and commands the greatest volume of air. With expansion of the ribs there must always be some contraction and descent of the diaphragm, or the full quantity of air would not enter the chest. This form of diaphragmatic breathing does not involve any distension of the lower part of the abdomen. On the contrary, full costal expansion with a forward movement of the triangular space between the ends of the short ribs (epigastric movement) actually diminishes it, as proved in practice by the flattening of the lower abdominal muscles.[1] When a full inspiration has been obtained in this manner voice should begin.

For expiration, which in the case of the singer is required to sustain and prolong the voice, the following forces are available:

(1) Elasticity of lungs—on relaxing the diaphragm.
(2) Abdominal muscular force — pressing the diaphragm upwards.
(3) Elasticity of lungs and chest-wall — on relaxing the rib-muscles.
(4) Depression of ribs.

[1] Opposition to the bulging at and below the *umbilicus* is offered by the *rectus abdominis*, and more particularly by its head.

If they acted together there would be a rapid emptying of the lungs as in ordinary breathing for action, in which elasticity plays the principal part. But to prolong the voice it becomes necessary to keep the breath forces under control. This is most easily effected by using them separately.

Number 2—the gentle retraction of the abdominal wall pressing the diaphragm upwards—can be safely used before the ribs are allowed to come down, and in well-developed breathing for voice the rib muscles relax only at the end of the period of voice-making.

By retaining the force of the ribs in reserve without stiffening or antagonistic action the air pressure is made even and continuous and the elastic tension of the expanded ribs supports the vocal pitch and favours resonance.

The following summary will make clear the objects which should underlie practice.

(1) The voice user requires flexibility of rib action for inspiration, and elastic tension of the ribs during expiration. General flexibility must be first established before practising exercises for control.

(2) The correct poise of the body is essential to control.

(3) The abdominal muscles play a definite part in controlling exaggerated abdominal inspiration and in timing correct and controlled expiration. They must therefore be made firm and flexible.

(4) Expiration must be carried on first by the upward movement of the diaphragm under the abdominal muscular force, while the ribs remain expanded.

There follow four exercises to help in developing these conditions preliminary to the production of the vocal note. (*See* Appendix I.)

The Note is the result of the vibrations of the vocal membranes, more commonly called the vocal cords. These act on the principle of a reed; producing vibrations as the result of breath passing through a narrow chink or slit.

This element of the note is the result of unconscious action under the indirect control of the ear, and the training of the ear should be begun by unaccompanied practice in very early childhood. No child should be allowed to remain tone-deaf. Psychologically there is no surer way of setting up a sense of inferiority, of divergence from one's fellows, of contempt for æsthetic and emotional expression in others, and finally of that antagonistic, anti-social isolation which is a danger to the individual and to the community.

Of this, surely, our own Shakespeare was thinking when he wrote his condemnation of

The man that hath no music in his soul.

No effort should be made to bring the production of the musical note under any control but that of the ear.

Tone is the result of the blended resonances of the cavities around and above the vocal membranes. We think of tone in terms of quality, duration and force. Quality is the result of:

(*a*) Perfect synchronising between the outward motion of the air and the instant of phonation (*i.e.* sounding of the voice). Too late drawing together of the membranes gives "breathy" tone: a closure of the membranes before the instant of impact with the air gives a sharp, plucking sound known as "shock of the glottis," or rough attack, which should never be heard in speech.

(*b*) Absence of all tightening in the muscles about the throat, *e.g.* the muscles of the tongue, palate, jaw

I

and lips. Contraction of the muscles above the note formed by the vibrating membranes gives

    i. Throaty tone, caused by undue depression or raising of the tongue, or

    ii. Nasal tone, caused by the meeting of the back of the tongue and the soft palate during the formation of sounds which are not intended to be nasalised. This term is also sometimes improperly applied to the complete cutting off of all nasal resonance, both in vowels and consonants.

(c) Unimpeded vibration from the initial note through the resonators to the shaped curve of the lips.

This is the final result of perfect synchronising of all the elements of breath, note and tone in the vowel shape.

Duration depends on the breathing control which has been described above. (*See* page 114, paragraphs 2 and 3.)

Force in like manner depends on the increase of breath pressure. (*See* page 112, paragraph 6.) But the use of both factors is extremely dependent on a mental sense of rhythm, and this again, as has been already indicated, should be one of the objects of a complete physical training in children, especially through the medium of dancing.

The following two rules, which have secured almost universal acceptance, relate to the relationship between vowel sounds and tone.

(1) The tongue-tip should never be drawn back from the lower front teeth in English vowel or diphthong sounds.

(2) The corners of the lips should never be drawn back beyond their natural width when at rest.

A detailed analysis of the vowel sounds themselves will be found in Chapter X., page 232.

The shapes of the resonator scale which are there indicated form a true " standard " of fundamental vowel formation, based on physiological and acoustic principles, as distinguished from the "received standard" of the phonetician, which is the result of a careful collation of averages among people not specially trained in good speech movement. It also differs from the artificial standard of the "elocution" or singing teacher derived from the traditional imitation of the mannerisms of past actors and singers; these are often short cuts to audibility without quality or conviction.

It is important to distinguish between formation and selection in vowel sound. An example may be given in the constant controversy between the two pronunciations *"either"* and *"eether."* This is a matter of selection, not of formation. It is therefore a question which should be determined purely by phonetic standard; by the practice of the majority of educated people.

" Ēpoch, ĕpoch " ; " Respīte, respit "; " Labòr'atry, làb'ratry," are other examples. Here the argument from derivation may be employed, but it is so often inconclusive in its operation that all we need consider is not to put ourselves "into the trick of singularity."

The observance of the two rules cited above, however, is not a question of selection, but of formation; here the decision should lie not with the phonetician, but with the phonologist or voice user; on the scientific basis of the resonator scale it will be found that these movements modify the fundamental vowel resonances, without resulting in a measurable distinction of vowel quality—a new vowel; that is to say they simply put the vowel out of tune, they do not raise or lower it to a new note.

Compare this with the case of musical pitch. If a piano tuner informed you that A^2 on your piano sounded at too rapid a rate of vibration, or in other words was slightly sharp, you would not answer, " Oh, I like it better sharp," or " Nearly all the pianos I have heard are slightly out of tune," or "It sounds strange to me me when you put it in tune." You would accept his judgment and have the note put right. In the same way when, on testing the respiratory resonances, *i.e.* the breathed sound of the vowel "o" (ou), the phonologist points out that it is too high in pitch, that its resonance has shifted too far in the direction of "e" (iı) because the tongue is raised, so destroying the proportion of the vowel scale and its capacity for pure resonance, it is not an answer to say, "Most people seem to me to make it like that"; you must first establish the fundamental intervals of the vowel resonator scale; afterwards, if you retain a preference for saying "eu" instead of "o" in words like "Oh, no," you can be dealt with by the phonetician, who will show you that you are deviating from "standard" beyond the point that is permissible. Personal affectations and peculiarities serve only to distract attention from what is being spoken and blur its significance.

It is important to realise that certain apparent errors in selection are in reality errors of formation: two examples will serve.

(1) The Cockney substitution of "aa" for "i," as in the variant of "Bahl Id Räad" instead of "Mile End Road," which is frequently adopted by the inhabitants thereof, is not a mere transliteration; not, that is to say, as the substitution of "tar" for "tire." The speaker aims at "i" and fails to achieve the necessary delicacy in movement for the production of the diphthong. He obtains a thick sound, either full of nasal twang, or com-

pletely devoid of nasal resonance, by the raising
of the tongue or the closure of the nasal passages.

(2) The substitution of "aw" (ɔː) for "o" (ɔ) in the
series off, officer, office, cough, coffee, gospel,
God. This is not substitution of the long sound,
clearly and accurately formed, for the short, not
the change of "cot" into "caught"; it is a
modification of "o" by a backward tongue-
movement, which makes the sound appear
approximately a badly formed "aw" but does
not quite achieve it.

Where an apparent error in selection is always accompanied by a markedly inferior vocal tone, and a generally
poor level of articulation, it may almost always be put
down as an error in formation.[1]

A test which seldom fails is to observe the effect of
a variation in different languages or dialects. For
instance, judging by English alone, it would be possible
to argue one of two things: either that nasal resonance
was always wrong in a vowel sound, or that Cockney
nasalisation was as good a way as any other of speaking,
and might prevail if a sufficient majority of people
came to adopt it.

But if we examine French diction we shall find the
four nasal sounds in

Un bon vin blanc

compatible with perfect tone, in fact adding a beauty
to it, and at the same time we shall learn from the
phonetician that these sounds do not exist in Standard
English. We shall, therefore, realise that it is possible
to use a large increase of nasal resonance without injury
to tone or vowel quality, but that where the use of
such resonance injures either, we are in the presence of

[1] Such modifications are in no sense "dialect"; it would be
as sensible to call a cold in the head a dialect.

an error in formation—nasal twang—and not of an error of selection. On the other hand we may also come to realise that the extremest form of Cockney results from the complete cutting off of nasal resonance.

A standard of formation can be and should be scientifically exact within certain definite limits.

A standard of selection, once exact formation has been established, should be a matter of purely phonetic selection, based possibly on a rather more careful study of the results of good formation than we can achieve at present.

The standard of selection is of vital concern to anyone who is acquiring a foreign language in adult life. In the mother tongue it should be acquired in childhood. The standard of formation concerns the whole future of a language as an instrument of æsthetic expression or of literary distinction.

Shakespeare in his "Speech to the Players" [1] lays the whole stress on formation, and elsewhere he shows an ear keenly sensitive to selection, with an intolerance of affectation in the choice both of vocabulary and pronunciation.

The lowest standard of speech we have to consider is therefore that of the ordinary educated speaker of English with no marked faults of voice or accent; it is in effect the standard English of the phonetician with a few modifications due to more exact formation as distinguished from selection.

It is interesting to recall Henri Bergson's description of such speech:

J'écoute deux personnes converser dans une langue inconnue. Cela suffit-il pour que je les entende? Les vibrations qui m'arrivent sont les mêmes qui frappent leurs oreilles. Pourtant je ne perçois qu'un bruit confus

[1] *Hamlet*, Act III. Scene ii.

où tous les sons se ressemblent. Je ne distingue rien et ne pourrais rien répéter. Dans cette même masse sonore, au contraire, les deux interlocuteurs démêlent des consonnes, voyelles et syllabes qui ne se ressemblent guère, enfin des mots distincts. Entre eux et moi, où est la différence?

La question est de savoir comment la connaissance d'une langue, qui n'est que souvenir, peut modifier la matérialité d'une perception présente, et faire actuellement entendre aux uns ce que d'autres, dans les mêmes conditions physiques, n'entendent pas. . . .

La difficulté serait insurmontable, si nous n'avions réellement affaire qu'à des impressions auditives d'un côté, à des souvenirs auditifs de l'autre. Il n'en serait pas de même si les impressions auditives organisaient des mouvements naissants, capables de scander la phrase écoutée, et d'en marquer les principales articulations. Ces mouvements automatiques d'accompagnement intérieur, d'abord confus et mal coordonnés, se dégageraient alors de mieux en mieux en se répétant; ils finiraient par dessiner une figure simplifiée, où la personne qui écoute retrouverait, dans leurs grandes lignes et leurs directions principales, les mouvements mêmes de la personne qui parle. Ainsi se déroulerait dans notre conscience, sous forme de sensations musculaires naissantes, ce que nous appellerons le schème moteur de la parole entendue. Former son oreiller aux éléments d'une langue nouvelle ne consisterait alors ni à modifier le son brut ni à lui adjoindre un souvenir; ce serait coordonner les tendances motrices des muscles de la voix aux impressions de l'oreille, ce serait perfectionner l'accompagnement moteur.[1]

In colloquial speech there is, then, a crushing synthesis of crowded syllables, advance only along the easiest succession of movements, elision of many unstressed vowels, poor vocabulary, no effort at verbal distinction, very little range of stress or phrasing.

Directly the subject-matter of speech becomes more unfamiliar, as in reading aloud or lecturing, a certain unfamiliarity of subject-matter and vocabulary compel

[1] BERGSON, *Matière et Mémoire*, page 143.

clearer and more measured speech because the hearer's motor memories no longer help him to "guess" so well.

Directly rhythmic patterns are added, as in measured prose or verse, the necessity for measuring the temporal succession of stresses and the duration of syllables arises.[1] In rhymed or assonant verse, stability of vowel quality must be attained.

Finally, in song the whole durational value of the vowel may be altered to fit the melody; the result of this will be illustrated in Chapter X.

It becomes clear that close study of such difficulties would restore our capacity for listening critically and with enthusiasm to beautiful speech, since as speech consists of motor memories the character of our own utterance is important in listening.

It is only as we ourselves have learnt the art of speech that we can read. It is only as we ourselves hear the music of words that we can reconstruct that music as we read. We see that the multiplicity of books and their cheapness and variety has deadened our faculty of hearing, has lowered the claim we make upon the music of speech in everyday life, and largely destroyed the executive skill of the dramatic artist in speech. We are only just escaping from a like bondage in lyric poetry ; and we must restore the power of rapid and exact hearing in dramatic audiences, if we are to have a renaissance of the spoken word in art, embracing to-day not a small and privileged class, but the whole nation.

We must give to our children a training which will ensure at each stage of their growth delight in personal experience of the beauty and significance of spoken sounds.

There is no surer agent of class antagonism than

[1] See Chapter VII. page 172.

the establishment of a definite "class standard" of accent and speech.

In considering the training of utterance we come now to clarity of logical expression.

Clarity is achieved first by articulation: that is to say by the sounds which result directly from the movements of the organs of speech. A small child can be watched acquiring these and practising, for the delight of both sound and sensation, a much larger range than those finally selected for use in language.

Properly considered, the shaping of the vowels by the lips and tongue is part of articulation, but the object of vowel shaping is to produce a stable resonance, passing as smoothly as possible into the following sound, and therefore modified by a slight glide in its final quality, as a vowel is the result of resonance in the mouth cavities, never, if it is rightly made, of any form of frictional noise. In the breath consonant, voice has been completely shut off, and the sound heard is purely frictional. Two nasal sounds, those represented by the letters "m" and "n," are in reality closed vowels; it will be more convenient therefore to limit the term "articulation" to those sounds where the sound is the result of movement rather than of stable position and vocal tone. In the following list the sounds italicised in the first four lines are vocal sounds, *i.e.* sounds formed by the resonance of the voice in certain cavities unaccompanied by a movement during utterance.

1. Main vowels: M*oo*(uː)t, M*oa*(ou)t, M*au*(ɔː)l, M*ar*(aː)t, M*a*(ei)te, M*ee*(iː)t.

2. Subordinate vowels : N*oo*(u)k, N*o*(ɔ)t, N*u*(ʌ)t, N*er*(əɪ)ve, Gn*a*(æ)t, N*e*(e)t, Kn*i*(ɪ)t.

3. Diphthongs: T*i*(ai)me, T*oi*(ɔi)l, T*ow*(au)n, T*u*(juː)ne.[1]

[1] The initial sound of this combination is y, not ee in ordinary speech.

4. Closed vowels: M(m)aize, N(n)ame.
5. Liquids: L(l)ake, R(r)ay.
6. Semi-vowels: Y(j)ield, W(ω)ake, Wh(hω)ey, Sing(ŋ).
7. Voice consonants: B(b)ed, D(d)ead, J(dʒ)est, G(g)uest, V(v)ie, Th(ð)en, Z(z)eal, Rouge(ʒ).
8. Breath consonants: H(h)ay, P(p)ay, T(t)ake, Ch(tʃ)ain, C(k)ape, F(f)ade, Th(θ)ane, S(s)ale, Rush(ʃ).

In line three, the diphthongs each consist of two such shapes blended together—the weaker of the two becoming at times almost consonantal in value. The succeeding five lines show in italics sounds in which the vocal element gradually diminishes until in the last line the sounds marked are completely non-vocal or, as we should say, whispered.

The ordinary classification of the phonetic alphabet will be familiar to almost everyone, and it can be found in two books on this subject,[1] but in speaking verse a slightly different classification will be of use because the nature of the consonants affects quantity through the duration of the syllables. From this point of view the sounds Y W V F R L NG TH (both sounds) and all the sibilants, S Z SH GE CH J, can be more or less prolonged in speech, while B P D T G K H WH are instantaneous in duration though often weighty in force. Considering the formation of the first series the following table will be of use.

Passage narrowed at	Lips	Teeth and Lips	Point and Blade	Front of Tongue	Palate and Back of Tongue
Voiced	W. V.	TH.	Z. GE.	J.	NG.
Voiceless	WH. F.	TH.	S. SH.	CH.	

[1] *Sounds of Spoken English* and *Good Speech*. W. Ripman.

"R." Point of tongue trilled, or breath passing over raised tip.

"L." Point of tongue touching palate.

"H." Whispered breath passing through the mouth.

There is also the final "R" sound which generally occurs as a modifier to the vowels (*see* line 2, No. 4), but which is sounded between two vowels by slightly raising the point of the tongue: compare

"bear it"

and

"bear them."

The second series is more easily followed, for it consists of positions in which breath or voice murmur are checked and heard on release.

Closure made by	Lips	Point of Tongue	Front or middle of Tongue
Voiced	B.	D.	G.
Voiceless	P.	T.	K.

These lists will make it clear that there are only ten sounds in English which completely cut off even a minimum of vocal sound. This fact is of the very greatest importance for the speaking of verse, for it means that vocal tone need be but rarely interrupted in lyric verse. In three such lines as:

Myriads of rivule*ts* *h*urrying *th*ro' the lawns,
The moan of doves in immemorial elms,
And murmuring of innumerable bees
(TENNYSON, *Princess*),

only the three sounds in italics ever interrupt the vocal vibration completely. This again emphasises the necessity of a perfect balance between voice and articulation

—a balance which is best achieved by the detachment of the one from the other so that they work like the two hands of the violin player, in perfect sympathy but in perfect individual independence. There is no excuse at any time in verse for the use of that hideous thing which is known phonetically as the "glottal stop." To use it is to admit that a succession of vowel or semi-vowel shapes cannot be carried through smoothly, but must at some moment imply a sharp closure of the vocal chords and a subsequent unco-ordinated action between them and the breath pressure. (*See* page 115.)

The form of succession in which this is likely to occur is in an ill-constructed cacophonous succession of vowels like these:

> And ere her ear had heard
> Her heart had heard.

In the effort to avoid

> Andare herear had hurd her heart'd hurd,

ill-trained speakers achieve

> And ᵊere her ᵊear hade . hearde
> Her . hearte hade . hearde.

The Greeks took great pains to avoid such successions, and what they called "hiatus," [1] the sharp succession of two staccato vowels; such a succession would occur in

> "A angel,"

and for this reason we use "an" before a vowel and harden "thŭ (ðə)" into "the (ði)."

> Thĭ (ði) ancients some and some thŭ (ðə) moderns praise.

---

[1] The hiatus is strictly prohibited in French verse, and rarely used even in comic drama.

> Gardez qu'une voyelle à courir trop hâtée
> Ne soit d'une voyelle en son chemin heurtée.
> BOILEAU, *Art Poétique.*

Poets further introduce elision where they feel the danger of too crowded syllables in their line. Milton's practice in this is the most weighty example. (*See* Chapter III. page 61.)

Examples:

> Than tir'd eyelids upon tir'd eyes.
>> TENNYSON, *Lotus Eaters*.

> Above th'Aonian Mount while it pursues.
>> MILTON, *Paradise Lost*, I. 15.

Again, this:

> Hell heard *the un*sufferable noise; hell saw
> Heaven ruining heaven and would have fled
> Affrighted.
>> MILTON, *Paradise Lost*, Book VI.

where the short vowel becomes almost equivalent to a "y" glide.

> Time*ly in*terposes and her monthly round.
>> MILTON, *Paradise Lost*, Book III.

A similar glide takes place with "w":

> Vert*ue in* her shape how lovely, saw, and pin'd.
>> MILTON, *Paradise Lost*, Book IV.

> Thou didst accept them; wilt th*ou en*joy the good?"

Discussion of all these compensating modifications will be found in Robert Bridges' *Milton's Prosody*,[1] where a wonderful delicacy of ear and poetic sense are coupled with a degree of scholarship and exactitude previously unknown in English metric study.

It is not the province of this book to give directions for acquiring correct speech in general. Poetry should not be used for linguistic gymnastics, though it is true

[1] *Op. cit.*, *cf.* page 61.

that the speaking of verse constantly and with distinction best re-creates the inner sense of the word-values,

> As those move easiest who have learned to dance.

But the faults which become apparent only in rhythmic delivery may be briefly summarised.

(1) The most important are those which concern the final, short unstressed vowels in terminations, or small unstressed words in rapid succession like "And to do, from by with, as in, forasmuch as, because, of course."

The list on pp. 138 and 139 is based on Dr. Aikin's Resonator Scale. The numbers at the top give the order of the sounds in that scale, which is more fully analysed in Appendix II.

In each case an example of the stressed form of the vowel and its phonetic symbol is given at the head of the column. In the lists various unstressed forms of the vowel are given without regard to the foolish and misleading forms of spelling.

In order to test the right pronunciation, a sentence in which the word is used in an unstressed or unemphatic form must be selected. Quotations illustrating this follow the list.

The effect of metric speech is to restore part of the vowel value to words commonly elided in ordinary speech.

The effect of sense emphasis falling on that particular word is to bring back a still greater degree of value to the vowel quality, but without necessarily lengthening the sound.

An untrained speaker will hesitate how best to accomplish this and often fall back on one of two expedients:

i. Speaking the word fully articulated as in the dictation of a list of single detached words.

ii. Pronouncing the word as it is spelt, *e.g.* "often" for colloquial "off'n."

Here are certain examples:

1. *Open*   colloquial   Op'n.

> "Will you op'n the door, please?"

> Opun, locks,
> Whoever knocks!
> > *Macbeth*, Act IV. Scene i.

Here the elided "e" would shorten the verse so that the right rhythm could not be achieved.

2. *Do.*   colloquial   "How d'y-dŏ?"

This is a meaningless phrase entirely pointed by vocal tone: no one dreams of answering the question; should we really want an answer we immediately add emphatically:

> "How *are* you?"

Emphatic speech:

> "Dōō get it for me."

> Thus thou must dōō if thou have it;
> And that which rather thou dost fear tŏ dōō
> Than wishest should be undone.
> > *Macbeth*, Act I. Scene v.

3. "You *should* be more careful."

> "You shood have seen!"

the word but not the vowel is long.

She shōōd have died hereafter ("oo" intermediate in length);
There would have been time for such a word.
> *Macbeth*, Act V. Scene v.

4. So in the case of syllabic "l":

"Will you blow a soap bubbl?"

Double, double, toil and trouble;
Fire, burn; and, cauldron, bubble.
Macbeth, Act IV. Scene i.

It is often sufficient in verse to give this restored quality to a vowel to secure the necessary emphasis, without lengthening, stressing, or vocally accenting the word by a change of pitch.

Now compare the whole list with the verse examples following.

I. and I.* (uɪ, u).

I have crowned her hair with the field flowers wild;
Cowslip, and crowsfŏot, and coltsfŏot bright.
ADAM LINDSAY GORDON, *Ballad of Britemarte*.

Then goat-fŏot marked the flying years.
E. PHILPOTTS, *The Faun that loved a Girl*.

And dearer yet the Brotherhŏod
That binds the brave of all the earth.
HENRY NEWBOLT, *Clifton Chapel*.

Glŏŏmy and beautifŭl alleys of trees arise.
W. B. YEATS, *Prothalamion*.

IV. and VI. (ɔ, ʌ).

"Make tŏ yourself friends of the Mammŏn of Unrighteousness,"
Plunged headlŏng down with flourished heels.
W. W. GIBSON, *The Ice Cart*.

Instead of the Crŏss, the Albatrŏss
About my neck was hung.
S. T. COLERIDGE, *Ancient Mariner*.

To carven rocks and sculptur'd promŏnt'ries.
FLECKER, *Brumana*.

And the overtŏppled chair.
W. W. GIBSON, *Flannen Isle*.

When Solŏmon was King.

> G. K. CHESTERTON, *Lepanto*.

Art may tell a truth ŏbliquely.

> ROBERT BROWNING.

Noon ŏn Oxford Town.

> FLECKER, *Dying Patriot*.

VI. (ʌ).

It was a mirăcle of rare device,
A sunny pleasure-dome with caves of ice.

> S. T. COLERIDGE, *Kubla Khan*.

Children of Tempest all ŭnshakĕn still.

> N. MUNRO, *To Exiles*.

Those shakĕn mists a space ŭnsettle.

> F. THOMPSON, *The Hound of Heaven*.

Strange, piteŏus, futile thing.

> F. THOMPSON, *The Hound of Heaven*.

To an opĕn house in the evening
Home shall men come.

> G. K. CHESTERTON, *The House of Christmas*.

And like the baseless fabric of this visiŏn.

> *The Tempest*, Act IV. Scene 1.

O world, unknowăble, we know thee.

> F. THOMPSON, *In no Strange Land*.

VII. (ə:).

To what green altăr, O mysterious priest,
Lead'st thou that heifĕr, lowing at the skies.

> KEATS, *Ode on a Grecian Urn*.

If this be errŏr, and upon me proved,
I nevĕr writ, nor no man evĕr loved.

> SHAKESPEARE, *Sonnet CXVI*.

So through the thundĕr comes a human voice.

> ROBERT BROWNING, *Saul*.

With glooming robes, pŭrpureal, cypress-crowned.

> F. THOMPSON, *The Hound of Heaven*.

K

VIII and VI. (æ, ʌ).

"Well I'm hungry."
"Oh, are you? I'm sorry, I'll fetch you some bread in
    a minute."
"*Bread*—dry bread? Oh, no!"
"And butter!"
"Bread 'nd butter Miss!"
HOUSMAN and BARKER, Prunella.

"And" is here fully articulated as in VIII., stressed
and then elided.

And—fled from monarchs, St. John, dwells with thee.
POPE, Essay on Man.

"And" is lengthened but not stressed; "und" is very
ugly.

They look at you with small, black, topăz-tinted eyes,
And wish you ill.
HARVEY, Ducks.

Topăzes, and cinnamon, and gold moidores.
MASEFIELD, Cargoes.

The long brook falling thro' the clov'n ravine
In catărăct after catărăct to the sea.
TENNYSON, Œnone.

Who is Silviă? what is she,
That all our swains commend her?
Two Gentlemen of Verona, Act IV. Scene ii.

Why, you may see
Imperial Agămemnon in the eyes
Of all his armăment walk daily forth
To take fresh note of sparrows and of snakes.
BRIDGES, Achilles in Scyros.

And now what monărch would not gard'ner be,
My fair Amandă's stately gait to see?
HOOKE, To Amanda.

He is crazed with the spell of far Arabiă.
WALTER DE LA MARE, *Arabia*.

In Xanădu did Kublă Khan
A stately pleasure-dome decree.
S. T. COLERIDGE, *Kubla Khan*.

Unpassioned beauty of a great măchine.
RUPERT BROOKE, *The Great Lover*.

IX. (e).

In stony Lebanon, where blooms
His red anemonĕ.
FLECKER, *Santorin*.

Inapprĕhĕnsible, we clutch thee.
F. THOMPSON, *In no Strange Land*.

The years had given them kindnĕss. Dawn was theirs.
RUPERT BROOKE, *The Dead*.

Your greennĕss on the heart's dĕspair.
H. TRENCH, *O Dreamy, Gloomy, Friendly Trees*.

If in thine ears their accĕnts linger.
ROBERT BROWNING.

And, oh, the foolishnĕss thou countest faith.
ROBERT BROWNING.

Let her ĕxcept . . . before accepted.
Twelfth Night, Act I. Scene iii.

XI. (i).

Respĭte, respĭte, and Nepenthe from thy memorĭes of
Lenore.
EDGAR A. POE, *The Raven*.

With short, sharp, violent lights made vĭvĭd
Only the swirl of the surges lĭvĭd.
ADAM LINDSAY GORDON, *The Swimmer*.

Mischĭĕf, thou art a-foot,
Take thou what course thou wilt.
Julius Cæsar, Act III. Scene ii.

Oh, world invisïble, we view thee,
Oh, world intangïble, we touch thee.

> F. THOMPSON, *In no Strange Land*.

Only the stuttering rifle's rapïd rattle
Can patter out their hasty orïsons,
No mockerïes for them.

> W. OWEN, *Anthem for Doomed Youth*.

And our peace is put ïn ïmpossïble things,
Where clashed and thundered unthïnkable wings
Round an ïncredïble star.

> G. K. CHESTERTON, *House of Christmas*.

My Indian bliss, my river-lïlÿ bud.

> KEATS, *Endymion*.

Second vowel in "lily" closer to IX. (e).

We do not detach our syllables as the French do, and in correcting these vowels care must be taken never to stress an unstressed syllable instead of retaining true vowel sound, as for instance "und" for "and." Note, however, that all unstressed vowels tend towards the indeterminate vowel vi. (ə).

(2) The transformation of "t" and "d" into "ch" and "j" in certain terminations is not permissible in verse.

"-tion," ("affection," "attention," etc.), is established, and must not be modified except possibly in one or two Shakespearean restorations. (*See* page 142.) But "tune," "Tuesday," "duke," "duty," "nature," "picture," "righteousness," can be restored in metric speech to their correct sound.

The objection to the use of "ch" and "j" is that an addition is thus made to the already excessive number of sibilant sounds in English. On the other hand the narrowing of these sounds into the long "u" ("pictūre," "natūre," etc.) is an error of genteel English which also gives us a minced formation of

"pin" for pen, "bed" for bad, "nace" for nice.

The colloquial effect of such affectations is intolerable in poetry.

(3) One cannot too strongly deprecate the effort to obtain emotional effect by modifying the vowel or consonant quality; "lauve" for love, "par-shun" for passion, "hearrt" for heart, "warr" for war, are all bombastic absurdities and simply get between the speaker and his audience.

Turning now to consonant sounds, the general importance of articulating terminal consonants like

t d p b k g f v,

is recognised. But there is a tendency to add a final mute "e" in emphatic words which is peculiarly unpleasant. "Dead" becomes "deade," and, in moments of great emotion, even "ted":

"Having kisseduh the womanuh ande lefte herre ted."
Perhaps this is more often sung than said. There remains the question of the habitual modification of certain words in poetry. Twenty years ago the list was a long one—it is now confined to a very few words.

Two modifications generally accepted in verse diction need consideration:

(a) The restoration of "h" in the combination "wh," the aspirate preceding the "w" in pronunciation.

> Why dost thou whet thy knife so earnestly?
>> *Merchant of Venice*, Act IV. Scene 1.

> Where the wind's like a whetted knife.
>> MASEFIELD, *Sea Fever*.

Both these lines are slightly humorous with the

omitted "h." The aspirate is being more generally used here than was the case a few years ago, and the tendency is to establish the rule in poetry that there are only four silent, written aspirates in English:

> heir, honest, honour, hour,

with the derivatives of the last three.

Uriah Heep killed "'umble" in the Church Service, but Medea still gathers her enchanted "'erbs" in Shakespeare's verse. (*Merchant of Venice*, Act V. Scene v.)

(*b*) The letter "r" presents grave difficulties to the English speaker. It has two initial sounds in English: fricative and trilled. The former is the result only of a momentary approximation of the tongue-tip to the flat surface immediately behind the upper front teeth: the second needs a quivering movement of the extreme tongue-tip caused by resistance to the outcoming breath. The former is generally used in colloquial speech—the second seems essential to the beauty of certain poetical lines:

> I run, I run, I am gathered to thy heart
> (ALICE MEYNELL, *Renouncement*),

where this line occurs as the climax of one of the most beautiful sonnets in English. The trilled "r" does not occur after "t" and "d."

Final "r" is only heard when followed by an initial vowel. This sound has the effect of reducing almost all the unaccented vowels to a uniform sound. (*See* column VII., page 138.)

It is an exaggeration to attempt to restore fricative or trilled "r" to the end of a word which is not followed by a vowel; this peculiar affectation used to be known as the "Surrey Theatre 'r'" from its adoption by melodramatic actors.

It is also questionable whether even in metric speech "aw" and "or" can be differentiated. The distinction gives a slight flavour of provincialism to speech. Yet it is valuable to practise this distinction as an exercise after "o," "ah," and "aw," because a clear perception of the alternate presence and absence of "r" helps to prevent the vulgarism of

"The pawr of the lion and the pawr of the bear,"
"The idear of it "—

errors which many educated southern English people unconsciously transfer to metric from colloquial speech, but which are never found in the speech of educated Scotch and Irish people who always give a slight, even if an almost imperceptible value to the consonant, though it is followed by a consonant.

(c) Besides these final consonants there is the difficulty of double initials:

cleanse, blood, strike, plunge.

Oh, blood, blood of Troy, etc.
The Trojan Women, Murray's trans.

In exaggerated dramatic diction, these consonants are sometimes divided and sustained—giving a most unpleasant effect.

And b-less the c-leansing fi-yer

is almost unbelievable, but might have been heard a very short time ago from one of our most popular singers.

Exaggeration of sibilant sound is much to be deprecated in English verse, particularly in syllables which carry a very heavy consonant charge. (*Cf.* Chapter X.)

Here is an example of this consonant charge, one of the difficulties of English lyric verse. It is taken from *Measure for Measure* and is deliberately used to weight

UNSTRESSED VOW

I*	IV	VI	
ŏo in took [u]	ŏ in top [ɔ]	ŭ in tun [ə]	ĕr i

shoŭld	ʃud	albatrŏss	ælbətrɔs	anemŏne	əneməni	altăr
coŭld	kud	buglŏss	bjuɪglɔs	Aarŏn	ɛərən	actŏr
dŏ	du	epŏch	iɪpɔk	bosŏm	buzəm	coloŭr
tŏ	tu	deadlŏck	dedlɔk	blossŏm	blɔsəm	errŏr
crowsfŏot	krouzfut	headlŏng	hedlɔŋ	commŏn	kɔmən	answĕ
logwŏod	lɔgwud	lavrŏck	lævrɔk	mirăcle	mirəkl	martў
manhŏod	mænhud	Cawdŏr	kɔɪdɔɪ	orăcle	ɔrəkl	satўr
				pigeŏn	pidʒ(ə)n	ochrĕ
				visiŏn	viʒ(ə)n	firĕ
				womăn	wumən	purĕ
				circumstănce	səɪkəmstəns	tirĕd
				chină	tʃainə	eăr
				Indiă	indiə	partic
Unstressed I		*Intermediate Sound*		Sylviă	silviə	regulă
ōo in mōod [uɪ]		armŏury	aɪməri	husbănd	hʌzbənd	ensure
Holyrōod hɔliruɪd		briŏny	braiəni	garlănd	gaɪlənd	
		priŏry	praiəri	dramă	draɪmə	
		mammŏth	mæməθ	islănd	ailənd	
		mammŏn	mæmən	ălas	əlɑɪs	
		balcŏny	bælkəni	Agămemnon	ægəmemnon	
				Leucotheă	ljukouθiɪə	
				opĕn	oupən	
				of(t)ĕn	ɔfən	
				frightĕn	frait(ə)n	
Stressed Forms		*Stressed Forms*		brightĕn	brait(ə)n	
				whistlĕ	hwis(ə)l	
dŏ	duɪ	wăs	wɔz	castlĕ	kɑɪs(ə)l	
tŏ	tuɪ			shăll	ʃəl	
				ănd	ənd	
				thĕ	{ ðə before cons. { ði ,, vowel	

NOTE.—The roman numerals refer to the resonator

VERSE AND SONG

VIII		IX		XI	
ă in tap [æ]		ĕ in ten [e]		ĭ in tin [i]	
abstrăct	æbstrækt	agăte	æget	flaccĭd	flæksid
catarăct	kætərækt	frigăte	friget	invĭsĭble	invizibl
almanăck	ɔɪlmənæk	magistrăte	mædjistret	horrĭd	hɔrid
topăz	toupæz	ĕnsure	enʃuɔ·	mischĭef	mistʃif
knapsăck	næpsæk	ĕxist	ĕgzist	tacĭt	tæsit
nomăd	noumæd	livĕst	livest	pencĭl	pensil
		sinnĕth	sineθ	sĭmĭle	simile
		vintăge	vintedʒ	respĭte	respit
		amĕthyst	æmeθist	vĭvĭd	vivid
		fountain	faunten	kerchief	kəɪtʃif
		captăin	kæpten		
		mountăin	maunten		
		marriăge	mæredj		
		bĕfore	befɔɪ		
		baselĕss	beisles		
		goodnĕss	guɪdnes		
		prophĕcy	prɔfesi		

Stressed Forms

shăll	ʃæl
ănd	ænd

Intermediate Sound

lilў	lili	(not liliɪ)
verў	veri	(,, veriɪ)
lilĭes	liliz	(,, liliɪz)
daisĭes	deiziz	(,, deiziɪz)
pitў	piti	(,, pitiɪ)

page 249), the guide words give the nearest stressed sound.

the utterance of a passage; it must not be confused
with syllabic length, as in the words

strung, cling, wrought,

for however numerous the consonants they should never
be sustained but touched off with sufficient rapidity,
not to interfere with the rhythm of the line, *i.e.* the
succession of its temporal accents. In order to do this
the tempo of such a line must be carefully adjusted.

Slow   Thou'rt not thyself;
      For thou exist'st on many thousand grains
      That issue out of dust: happy thou art not;
      For what thou hast not, still thou striv'st to get,
      And what thou hast forget'st. Thou art not certain;
      For thy complexion shifts to strange effects
      After the moon.

Measure for Measure, Act III. Scene i.

The same effect in rapid time gives a humorous impression:

Rapid   Great rats, small rats, lean rats, brawny rats,
      Brown rats, black rats, grey rats, tawny rats,
      Grave old plodders, gay young friskers,
      Fathers, mothers, uncles, cousins,
      Cocking tails and pricking whiskers,
      Families by tens and dozens—
      Brothers, sisters, husbands, wives,
      Followed the Piper for their lives.

ROBERT BROWNING, *Pied Piper*.

In all these consonants speech defects of a marked
type are fairly prevalent, but these should receive cura-
tive treatment before any attempt is made to speak verse.

There remains the question of certain words which
have traditionally been given a special poetic pronunciation.

Up till about twelve years ago the "i" in "wind"
was generally long in poetry simply for convenience of

rhyme; now poets ask us, even where it is so used, to make it an "eye rhyme" in order to avoid the sense of strangeness in poetic speech.

They say, and rightly, that words and pronunciations which have become "poetised," *i.e.* of exclusive use in poetry, lose their power to move, their associations becoming conventional, and on this ground they deprecate

O Wind,
If Winter comes, can Spring be far behind?
SHELLEY, *Ode to the West Wind.*

But they cannot expect the advantage of both methods, and must select their rhyme in accordance with the pronunciation they wish to adopt, despite Orlando's bad example:

> From the east to western Ind
> No jewel is like Rosalind,
> Her worth, being mounted on the wind,
> Through all the world bears Rosalind,
> All the pictures fairest lin'd
> Are but black to Rosalind,
> Let no face be kept in mind
> But the face of Rosalind.
>> *As You Like It*, Act III. Scene ii.

Some years ago Sir Johnston Forbes-Robertson fluttered the dovecotes by demanding the invariable poetic use of "agen" for "again." Investigation showed rhymes with "men," "then," etc., to have predominated in older use, those with "pain" in modern verse. But Shakespeare writes:

> But my kisses bring again,
>> Bring again.
> Seals of love, but seal'd in vain,
>> Seal'd in vain
>>> (*Measure for Measure*),

which is surely conclusive that both uses should be allowed.[1]

The Shakespearean archaisms stand on a different footing.　Mr. William Poel pleads for their retention, and in such matters his word should be law.

> That sweet aspèct of Princes
> And our ruin.

> When thy canònized bones hearsèd in death.

> As in a vault and ancient rèceptàcle.

> I'll wipe away all trivial recòrd.

> And make him full of hateful phantasȳès.

> This shows a true affechyone (affekshyōne).

The two last may be deprecated as likely to make even "the judicious" smile.　Those endings whch have become completely contracted can be balanced by verse line pause as:

> Bè not her màid—sìnce she is ènvious,

not

> Be nòt her màid since shè is ènvioùse.

The latter seems too metric for a modern ear.　Stressed "ed" as in Juliet's "Banishèd" is metrically necessary and must not be slurred.　*Cf. Romeo and Juliet:*

> Hence-banishèd is banish'd from the world,

where both forms are shown.

The object of all such niceties of restoration should

---

[1] In poetry both pronunciations are often used by the same writer;　thus Keats, Tennyson, Kipling and Bridges let *again* rhyme with *men, then, when,* and with *plain, slain, rain.*　William Watson has the rhyme *against: fenced.　Thames* is found in rhyme with *gems* (Bridges), as well as with *acclaims* (Tennyson).

WALTER RIPMAN, *The Sounds of Spoken English.*

be clarity. If at any time they are so exaggerated as to come between the audience and their absorption in the beauty of the verse or the content of the poem they are, to me, mischievous. But the other consideration also holds good; we have no right to irritate the sensitive ear of the scholar by neglecting the true value of a word or syllable through carelessness or self-conscious fear of pedantry.

> The censure of the which one must, in your allowance, o'erweigh a whole theatre of others.
>
> *Hamlet*, Act III. Scene ii.

The second element in clarity is significant emphasis. In ordinary speech this instinctively follows sentence structure: in verse we are faced with a conflict between metric stress and significant emphasis. The perfect blending of the two gives us rhythm; that is the synchronising of force, time, and spacial movement *under the direction of intention*.

It is plain that the logical structure and significance of a poem, what we call its meaning, is essential to the poet's intention quite as much as its metric structure or form. They were one in the poet's imagination. If he has accomplished his purpose it should be impossible to separate them in utterance.[1]

But the public often reads a poem as it looks at an Academy picture; with one eye on the title in the catalogue, merely to find out "what it is about." There is, therefore, a tendency to think only of the story or subject of a poem—or only of the dramatic excitement it can set up. People who speak verse like this allow their emphasis to destroy the tune of the poem and should never attempt anything but prose. They do not as a result become more but rather less significant,—

[1] *Cf.* Chapter VII on Prosody.

because the poet, as he wrought the words of his poem, brought out and fixed immutably many exquisite gradations of meaning which escape altogether when the words are over-emphasised.

There are three ways of marking emphasis:

    i. A greater degree of force on a word or syllable: this may occasionally conflict with metric stress.

    ii. A prolongation in the duration of the word or syllable: this may alter the quantity of a vowel.

    iii. Rise or fall in voice pitch: this must be very sparingly used in verse, except in drama.

Take as examples:

    i. I spràng to the stìrrup, and Jòris, and hè;
       I gàlloped, *Dirck* gàlloped, we gàlloped all thrèe.
                R. BROWNING, *Good News from Ghent.*

Here the stress on "Dirck" must be very slight if we are not to lose the lilt of the line.

    ii. One half of me is yours, the other half yours,
       Mine own, I would say; but if mine, then yours,
       And so all youers. O, these naughty times
       Put bars between the owners and their rights!
       And so, tho' yours, not youers.
                Merchant of Venice, Act III. Scene ii.

Another instance of Shakespeare's absolute unity of form and meaning.

    iii. Where grows? where grows it not! if vain our toil,
        We ought to blame the culture, not the soil.
                POPE, *Essay on Man.*

It is obvious how dangerous this method would be in lyric poetry.

The chief error made in emphasis is the substitution of metric for significant stress as in the child's sing-song. Elementary as this error seems, it is extraordinarily persistent: the best cure is a study of prosody on modern lines, recognising that, as in music only very occasionally will a bar be found in which no notes occur beyond those indicated in the time signature:

so in poetry the line admitting of exact syllabic scansion forms the exception; a succession of such lines would be intolerably monotonous in a language like English, where stress is strongly marked. In French, syllabic regularity is compensated by variety in stress. (*Cf.* Chapter III., page 66.)

No rules or directions can therefore dispense the reader in practice from the most exact study of significance. All English metric stresses are true sense-stresses, and those which appear to disobey this rule must be rejected. When these conditions have been fulfilled the following suggestions will be found useful:

i. Stress the verb in preference to the noun.

ii. In stressing the adjective, if it should be necessary, always carry the stress through into the noun.

iii. Except in the case of antithesis never stress connectives or adverbs.

iv. In verse with a strong accentual beat or lilt, emphasis may more safely be marked by voice variety.

v. In lyric, emphasis must never disturb the temporal fall of the stresses, and must never be stronger than the force of a verse stress. If stronger emphasis is urgently required it should be given by duration, that is to say by dwelling on the emphatic word.

vi. In dramatic verse the principle of verbal unity and sentence-form must be sought for in every passage. Sentences must not be broken into words or words into detached syllables.

vii. In categories or long cumulative successions of clauses the emphasis of individual words must be strictly subordinated to climax, and the growing intensity of the passage must be carried through the verse stresses as well as the emphatic words.

viii. All emphatic pauses must be kept within the limit of the temporal structure of verse in lyric poetry. In dramatic poetry this movement may be sparingly relaxed.

ix. No change of tempo, *i.e.* rate of speed, may be introduced in lyric verse which is not indicated in the metrical scheme.

x. In dramatic verse change of tempo is frequently required for the sake of differentiating character: if so, it must be sufficient to make a clear break in the metrical speed of the two groups of lines.

> *Hor.* My lord, I think I saw him yesternight.
> *Ham.* Saw who?
> *Hor.* My lord, the king your father.
> *Ham.* The king my father!
> *Hor.* Season your admiration for a while
> With an attent ear.
>
> *Hamlet*, Act I. Scene ii.

xi. Lines divided between two speakers should be given harmonious or definitely opposed emphasis.

> *Oliv.* Now, sir, *what* is your *text*?
> *Vio.* Most sweet lady——
> *Oliv.* A comfortable doctrine, and much may be said of it. Where *lies* your text?
> *Vio.* In Orsino's bosom, etc.
>
> *Twelfth Night*, Act I. Sc. v.

xii. Deliberate breaches in these rules must justify themselves by their effect on the emotional excitement apparent in the poet's verse—not as a mere relief to the speaker's physical or temperamental incapacity.

Where the artist has acquired the power to carry out the technical suggestions made in this chapter, and in addition is fundamentally gifted by mental and emotional capacity, we are in presence of the art which has probably the greatest power to move humanity of any known to us. An art which finds its medium in exquisite speech, in oratory, and in lyric or dramatic singing, as well as in verse, diction and dramatic speech.

The reaction of such training on the race has always been enormous; historically Greece, Italy, and France have been profoundly influenced by it, and its attainment was the object of a great part of mediæval classical training, and the acknowledged aim of the university dramatic performances which were an obligatory part of Elizabethan education.

The neglect of any such training has produced curious anomalies amongst us: the acquisition of a comical, pedantic or official speech by teachers and clergy, of a senseless and sounding rhetoric by orator and actor, of disintegrating social accents by different classes of the community.

All suggestions as to formal training must be held subject to these qualifications: The first condition of any technical training is the development of physical control through rhythm. The whole mechanism of utterance—breathing, voice, vowel formation, articulation—must be rhythmic; that is to say, able to measure unconsciously and spontaneously the spacial character, force and duration of every audible movement made; it must express thought in action.

L

The instrument which is used for rhythmic delivery must be fully capable of rhythmic action.

To be troubled in regard to the duration of the breath, the pitch or quality of the voice, to be conscious of uncertainty in regard to pronunciation, or lack of clarity in articulation—to have to think of any of these things when the mind should be consciously concerned only with the significance of the poem, and when the emotional beauty and the significance of the verse ought to show through the speaker's whole utterance, is to fail as an interpreter of poetry—to fail to express intention in action.

Even where the speaker is happily unconscious of his defects, and enjoys himself very much, the hearer will receive meaningless or irritating impressions and will be apt to conclude that they are due to the poet and not to his interpreter.

It must be repeated once again, the speaker *is* serving as an interpreter—clarifying what the reader cannot take in for himself, what the average individual may not have sufficient mental or emotional alertness to grasp. What the audience have already learned to love and what they delight to hear repeated, he must render with perfect transparency of meaning and expression. His primary object should never be to exploit his personality.

CHAPTER VI

EARLY TRAINING

In his beautiful introduction to *The Way of Poetry* John Drinkwater puts before us one side of a child's love of poetry. It is part of their pleasure in making things; making things very exactly and clearly in their own minds.

> The poet sees or understands something very clearly indeed, so clearly that he is able to put it quite clearly into his poem, and then in a wonderful way we make it all over again for ourselves in our own minds.
>
> *Introduction.*

Robert Lynd, in his introduction to another anthology, says that every child is a poet from the age at which he learns to beat a silver spoon on the table in numbers. Each writer has felt a part of the child's delight in poetry.

There is the almost physical delight in rhythmic pattern which makes a little child arrange everything he can get hold of into some kind of design; there is a delight in movement for its own sake and particularly in movements that make a noise; on the other hand there is profound curiosity about everything in life and a desire to make, to imitate, to create.

All the nursery rhymes in the world grew out of these fundamental instincts. The learning of these things is a child's earliest æsthetic education; dancing, dramatic expression in movement, the control of utterance, these are his first works of art, and with

149

them song, in which, if he be properly nurtured, he can acquire capacities which seem little less than magical to his elders. If full play were given to the natural rhythmic development of the individual it would place the mind in command of the body in such a manner that growth and education would progress in harmony.

The art of dancing must unquestionably be placed first in point of order; with it should come the lilt of words and of tunes, nursery rhymes, action songs and those delightful verses where the pitch of syllables follows the metric pattern instead of the speech inflection of the voice.

[1] Far and few, far and few

Are the lands where the Jumblies live.

Their heads are green

And their hands are blue,

And they went to sea in a sieve.

EDWARD LEAR.

Grasshoppers four a-fiddling went,

Heigh-ho! never be still!

[1] No attempt is made to indicate actual pitch, but the stresses must be marked softly by rising or falling tones according to the notes above or below the line.

They earned but little towards their rent

But all day long with their elbows bent

They fiddled a tune called Rilloby-rilloby,

Fiddled a tune called Rilloby-rill.

Minor key

Ah, but nobody now replied,

Heigh-ho! never be still!

When day went down the music died,

Grasshoppers four lay side by side,

And there was an end of their Rilloby-rilloby,

There was an end of their Rilloby-rill.

HENRY NEWBOLT.

It cannot be too often repeated that absolute spontaneity of expression is obtainable in a child. Psychologically, this possession is so priceless that no teaching must ever be allowed to jeopardise it. Therefore the child must have before it the very best and most perfect examples for the *unconscious* cultivation of taste in speech.

Poetry is an end in itself: it should never be used as a vehicle for teaching other things. And so from one point of view, children delight in nonsense and are very impatient of too much explanation. We have all heard of the child who said, "Oh, I could understand it so well if only she wouldn't explain it." But Mr. Drinkwater is also right in appealing to the child's intense desire to know the world in which he finds himself, and his wonderful grave delight in beautiful poems which are far too grown-up—so the grown-up think—for him to understand. Natural love and appreciation can be a sufficient substitute for adult understanding in all imaginative art. The most exquisite poems of childhood in English were written by that great mystic, William Blake, and in them we hear the very speech of a child's wistful wonder about life and about God.

> Little lamb, who made thee?
> Dost thou know who made thee,
> Gave thee life and bade thee feed,
> By the stream and o'er the mead;
> Gave thee clothing of delight,
> Softest clothing, woolly, bright;
> Gave thee such a tender voice,
> Making all the vales rejoice?
> Little lamb, who made thee?
> Dost thou know who made thee?
>
> Little lamb, I'll tell thee;
> Little lamb, I'll tell thee.
> He is callèd by thy name,
> For He calls Himself a Lamb;
> He is meek and He is mild,
> He became a little child.

I a child and thou a lamb,
We are callèd by His name.
  Little lamb, God bless thee!
  Little lamb, God bless thee!
                    WILLIAM BLAKE.

Almost everything is romantic to a child; it is not a very long step from

She has rings on her fingers and bells on her toes,

to

I will make you brooches and toys for your delight,
Of bird-song at morning and star-shine at night.
I will make a palace fit for you and me
Of green days in forests and blue days at sea.
                    R. L. STEVENSON, *Romance*.

Most children like to move when they are speaking jingles and nonsense rhymes. It seems to strengthen their muscular pleasure in speaking to a rhythmic pattern—just as they like to sing and dance together. But they do not like very much sense-emphasis in the lines they speak; they would rather sing-song the metre: and when they speak a poem which really appeals to them, if they know and love you well enough to let you hear, they like to stand very still and the only expression they show is that of their own shy delight in what they are speaking.

But they also love acting a poem, especially when they reach the stage of real story-telling—of ballad poetry; then they will make a play out of a ballad story or mime a ballad in dumb show with the greatest delight. It seems to me that we have here implicit in the child's mind all the formal growth of poetry—epic, lyric and dramatic—and that mischievous pleasure which underlies one part of what is called satyric poetry —for all children will jingle a "neck-verse" to tease one another on the model of Mr. Lear or "Mary, Mary, quite contrary."

I am convinced that children should be allowed to act and to tell stories with all the movement they like to use. But it is quite easy in lyric verse to get them to see the value of standing still "so that we may listen better." Only one thing they may not have: taught gesture of a deliberate kind; especially not that terrible referential gesture which performs a kind of dumb-crambo accompaniment to the poet's words.

Up to the age of seven all normal children possess a good memory, and I am convinced that if they are not allowed and encouraged to use it a very early age, the faculty wastes and is never so clear or so spontaneous again. To-day we very naturally distrust the mis-chievous old practice of cramming young children with strings of irrelevant facts, tables, dates, categories, etc., but modern education quite seriously fails to make use of this invaluable early gift and the gift declines when it is not used.

No vocabulary-learning gives a child the slightest trouble at that age. Languages are acquired quite unconsciously, poems can be learned almost at a hearing, and most intelligent children, if their time is not frit-tered away for them, will teach themselves to read by eye-memory before the age of seven. I do not believe that any one of these things puts a strain on a child's faculties—they simply form a delightful and engrossing game. No child ought, however, to need any form of corrective training in movement or utterance till after the age of seven. Then the period of second dentition and sudden growth in height takes place—temporarily upsetting the balance between growth, muscular strength and organic development.

It is at this period that nearly all speech failures

show themselves; it is then that stammering begins; and the difficulty of accommodating speech to the new dentition sets up various semi-nervous forms of lisping and lalling. It is above all necessary to say that any corrective training children need at this time should not be mixed up with the actual teaching of poetry. It is infinitely better and more amusing to construct a few simple general exercises which will improve the whole standard of speech, rather than to make the child word-conscious when reading or speaking. In every technical exercise there must be a delightful effort for achievement; for an easy measure of effort is the greatest delight to a child; he would rather run than walk, climb than march along level ground, catch or strike a ball than keep his hands in his pockets; speak quickly than mouth or drawl ; repeat catches than read words of one syllable.

Again, that delight in quick, rhythmic repetition, which would weary any grown-up, can be used for practice, and a child rejoices in any small piece of apparatus which may become a permanent possession. Exercises Nos. 1 and 2 (p. 252) in Appendix II. are illustrative of the type of exercise which a child will enjoy at this time.

Mr. H. Cooke has utilised the child's love of movement in a very remarkable manner to teach the fundamental principles of metre; he calls his exercises "flag-wagging" and arranges a rough outline of rhythmic beating, following, not the exact scansion or fundamental beat of the verse — which, when it can be disentangled, would be unvarying like time-counting in music—but the actual succession of syllables and accents in the line. I fear I am a little doubtful about the result of all these methods. Children find force easy, duration difficult, and spacial movement even more difficult, to measure. I question whether it is wise to attempt anything like analytical study until an age when reason begins to develop; when critical faculty becomes dominant too soon it is difficult to provide it with legitimate food.

The period of adolescence is the period of self-consciousness; associated as it is with marked changes in the mechanism of the voice, that self-consciousness very often concentrates itself on speech, and the sensitiveness which results makes all dramatic work or verse-speaking extraordinarily difficult. If early teaching has carried the child on by imitation to a point quite beyond its own natural range of expression, there will happen at this period the most violent revulsion against any æsthetic or emotional expression whatsoever. The only exception will be found among children of a weak and vain mentality, whose love of "showing off" will be stimulated by the advent of sex consciousness. It is from this latter class that the stage-struck in early youth are recruited; in class-teaching their external facility of expression and quick imitative powers may give them a superficial success, which still further disgusts the normal, healthy-minded boy or girl with the whole art of expression.

Even children with a touch of genius often become so profoundly discontented with their work at this stage that they will refuse to go on working at what they do best. Yet repression is equally dangerous. I suggest that it is then that a genuine beginning in technique should be made; clear and musical speech, intelligent diction, and the understanding of poetic form, will add a new interest to the fifteen-year-old's appreciation of poetry. Then there is the study of words; the sense that poetical thought is clearer, more concentrated, more exact, than prose—all that study of meaning in poetry which will destroy the comfortable theory of the "inspired idiocy" of the poet and show him to us as the seer and creator.

The child's first introduction to great lyric poetry should come at this period, for there, as John Drinkwater is always reminding us,

> The poet when he has finally chosen and arranged his words, if his poem is worth reading at all, has already said completely what he had to say, and if we add to his perfect expression this other feeble expression of our own, it is nothing but an impertinence, as though we were saying, "This poet is not able to express himself very clearly, so we must help him out."
>
> Words to the poet are what paint is to the painter, or stone or marble to the sculptor, or notes of sound to the composer of music.
>
> JOHN DRINKWATER, *The Way of Poetry*.

This is the age when personal taste in children begins to develop; the narrow limits of academic standards are cramping to the boy or girl who is finding out a way to self-expression, poetry is fading into the background at this time with many children, and they are feeling after the vocational capacity which later they must acquire in order to live. If they are presented only with examination selections, if poetry is not related to life as they know it, it will pass out of their active interest, and all their days they will miss something. If they are badly taught we shall hear that they cannot "stand that sort of stuff;" better not teach at all, but leave them to browse and discover with a thrill of astonishment what they really like. But if every teacher were as he should be, a speaker of pure and beautiful English, and if every teacher of English could read and speak verse and have some love of poetry, I do not believe even this temporary revulsion would be felt.

The reserve of adolescence will take pleasure, as I

have said, in simple lyric delivery, avoidance of gesture, avoidance of great inflectional variety, concentration on the significant music of words; but one must also insist on the danger of chaunted or arbitrarily monotonous delivery. One must ask for a careful following of every rhythmic indication. It is here that I value and use the word "diction"—that which the French call "l'art de dire"—the art of saying verse. I shall suggest presently that the very best medium for training it is comedy—that delicate, light, satyric verse in which we still lag far behind the literature of France.

I mean by "diction" that speech which results when after following the poet as truly as we can through his own path in the making of a poem, after thinking in pictures, and thinking in form, we think in words: feeling their musical significance, charged with association, tenderness and beauty, and when by our own gift of utterance we waken response to all this in our hearers.

Ballad poetry appeals most forcibly to boys and girls at the period of strong revolt from sentimentality. Ballad metre tends to a rather rigid regularity: a quatrain in alternate rhymed lines—the third often left blank—with alternate four and three accents:

> He's moùnted hèr on a mìlk-white steèd;
> And himsèlf on a dàpple grèy,
> With a bùglet hòrn hung dòwn his sìde;
> And lìghtly they ròde awày.
>
> *The Douglas Tragedy.*

But the rhythmic tune set to this time signature is of an incredible variety:

> They hàdna saìl'd a leàgue, a leàgue,
> A leàgue but bàrely thrèe,
> When the lìft grew dàrk, and the wìnd blew loùd,
> And gùrly grèw the seà.

. . . .

Half-òwre, half-òwre to Aberdoùr,
'Tis fìfty fàthoms deèp;
And thère lies goòd Sir Pàtrick Spèns,
Wi' the Scòts lords at his feèt!

Sir Patrick Spens.

Or compare the rhythmic values of each of the three
verses of the following poem:

Quinquireme of Nineveh from distant Ophir,
Rowing home to haven in sunny Palestine,
　　With a cargo of ivory
　　And apes and peacocks,
Sandalwood, cedarwood, and sweet white wine.

Stàtely Spanish gàlleon còming from the Ìsthmus,
Dìpping through the Tròpics by the pàlm-greèn shòres,
　　With a càrgo of diàmonds,
　　Èmeralds, àmethysts,
Tòpazes, and cìnnamon, and gòld mòidòres.

Dìrty Brìtish còaster wìth a sàlt-càked smòke-stàck,
Bùtting thròugh the Chànnel in the màd Màrch dàys,
　　With a càrgo of Tỳne còal,
　　Ròad ràils, pìg lèad,
Fìrewòod, ìronwàre, and chèap tìn tràys.

JOHN MASEFIELD, *Cargoes.*

One peculiarity of the ballad needs to be noticed in
speaking; every ballad begins, as it were, full blast:

The King sits in Dunfermline Town,
Drinking the blude-red wine.

Sir Patrick Spens.

I Catherine am a Douglas born,
A name to all Scots dear.

ROSSETTI, *King's Tragedy.*

They shot him dead by the nine-stane rig,
Beside the headless cross.

SURTEES, "Barthram's Dirge," *The English Poetry Book.*

White founts falling in the courts of the sun,
And the Soldan of Byzantium is smiling as they run.
                    G. K. CHESTERTON, *Lepanto*.

The murmur of the mourning ghost
That keeps the shadowy kine,
" O, Keith of Ravelston,
The sorrows of thy line! "
                    DOBELL, *Keith of Ravelston*.

The object was to arrest immediate attention: picture the conditions of some mediæval castle hall when the well-known story of some clan hero was sung or chaunted to while away the long fire-lit evening. Only those songs which could claim instant attention and keep their audiences awake by unflagging interest could hope to survive.

Anthologies of lyric poetry are so numerous and so excellent at the present time, that it is hardly necessary to give advice on the selection of poems. A little book on miming will follow this, and perhaps show to some a new method of rhythmic expression. One thing is difficult, the choice and selection of suitable ballads. There are not more than about twenty of our older ballads really possible for a child's speaking. Many are too long and many too gruesome, many deal with topics which do not concern children, but among our modern poets we have Newbolt, Chesterton, Kipling, and single poems by numberless singers. Sir Henry Newbolt's *Book of Ballads* contains a wonderful selection, to which might be added Flecker's "Brian of Brittany," "The Story of Kate Barlass," from *The King's Tragedy* by D. G. Rossetti, and Adam Lindsay Gordon's "How we beat the Favourite."

The genius of England has pre-eminently expressed itself in poetry and in great dramatic literature, not in music, not even in painting or sculpture. Yet the present generation has seen no faintest shadow of official recognition for the theatre; where alone dramatic art can come into being. It would be well at this stage to educate the next generation so that they may understand and remedy this.

The dramatic instinct in little children is best trained through play-making, and therefore does not come particularly within the scope of this book, though I have already said something about it in regard to epic poetry. But there should be one moment in a child's study of poetry which is memorable beyond all others —that is the moment when he first begins to love Shakespeare.

Individual character must determine the best way of making this momentous introduction. To some it comes through the medium of the stories, perhaps the least interesting part of the plays to us, though they must have interested Shakespeare or he would not have chosen them. To others it comes through songs, scenes, or even possibly sometimes (though I doubt this) through passages from the plays learnt by heart. But I believe the best way is to find a means of making Shakespeare's people come alive and become personal friends. Then everything they say or do will be interesting; for we love everything that concerns our friends; talk about them as if they were real people and as early as possible let them be real in the theatre. The late Canon Ainger once said to one of his students in literature who was seeking for advice about the education of her little daughter, "If you have the chance of taking her to see Shakespeare played in a *barn*, take her." In later years the command was literally obeyed in an Irish village where Hamlet and Ophelia might have been observed painting the scenery on the shady side of the building preparatory to the evening's performance.

It is a great pity to wait too long before seeing Shakespeare acted; for once the critical faculty begins to outpace the imaginative we cease to surrender ourselves to impressions, and often reject what is good because we cannot stomach its alloy of human failure. From this grows the futile academic attitude towards Shakespearean representation which we are now outgrowing, but which has been strong enough in the past to rob us of a National Theatre and to leave the majority of our boys and girls ignorant of their greatest national heritage.

In the acting of Shakespearean plays young people will learn more of themselves, of their own ability for team-work, for individual expression, and for initiative, than by any other method known to us. I have watched the effect of these performances in the same schools on successive generations of children for over twenty years: I have never seen a bad result of any kind; I have hardly ever known a boy or girl go out from them without a true love and understanding of Shakespeare. But of one thing I am certain: there are only two ways of doing a Shakespeare play in school. One is to leave the children entirely alone and accept what they can give at their own standard. The other is to make the production of a Shakespeare play the central artistic activity of the school for one term in the year, and, allowing for the students' ages, to get as beautiful, as critical, and as finished a performance as any artists can give. The first is extraordinarily interesting and works in well with modern free-period methods; the second requires the co-operation of a trained teacher. I have no doubt in my mind that it is the most valuable experience young people can go through in the course of their educational trainng. The tradition of such performances has lingered with us from Elizabethan days and it should everywhere be renewed. But the half-way method is detestable; it has neither spontaneity nor the charm of finish and style, it leads to nothing but self-satisfaction and stage-struck vanity.

If the suggestions made in this section are to be carried out it will be essential that a high standard of speech and a good knowledge of the vocabulary and pronunciation of English should be established throughout the school. How can this be accomplished without too great a sacrifice of time and effort?

It must be recognised in the first place that such a standard, once it is established, means an enormous saving of time in correction in all classes where English is the medium of expression, as well as rapid advance in capacity for the study of other languages, and in general self-expression. It means better class-answering, fewer "howlers," easier corrections.

The simplest and best method is of course the presence on every school staff of one expert in speech-training who can be made responsible for the general improvement of speech throughout the school. Where this is possible students can be graded in three main divisions. First the general mass of average speakers and readers with no very marked accentual or physical difficulties. Then those students whose speech is markedly below the average in either of these respects; finally the smaller group of students who show a definite talent for dramatic or lyric expression and who should therefore receive an artistic training in this direction if they are to develop naturally, in accordance with their personal gift of appreciation.

The first class need one period of class-training a week in which they will work progressively at speech and reading till they can pass a sufficiently severe test

M

in sight-reading, and rank as speakers of good standard English. This training should be first vocal, then phonological and phonetic, and afterwards linguistic; that is to say aiming at a good word-content, good sentence-structure, phrasing and logical analysis of sentences.

The second group need individual teaching, either singly or in carefully selected groups of two or three. And this teaching must continue for two or three years without interruption, and with constant reference to the general progress of the student in ordinary English subjects. The dangerous psychological effect of bad speech on mental development is still everywhere underestimated.

The third section should begin with the general voice- and speech-training given throughout the school, but as soon as they can reach a definite standard in ordinary speech they should be given careful individual training in verse-speaking and in a higher standard of diction.

The best method of grading is a reading test consisting of an unseen passage given throughout the school once a year. The grades may be divided into A, B and C groups, and these again subdivided into three sections. Not five per cent. of the students would attain to A1, and no grade should be given under twenty-five per cent. of the total marks.

After about three sessions of careful revision such a register of grades will begin to establish a definite standard throughout the school. No student over fourteen showing marked difficulties should be excused special speech work till they obtain a reasonable "C" grade, and no student should drop the general speech lesson till they are in an "A" grade.

The passages chosen are generally of about two minutes' reading length. Many good prose anthologies exist, but passages from essays serve well for the "A" grades, while the "B" grade may read from good novels and the "C" grade from such delightful books as Kenneth Grahame's *Golden Age* or Kipling's *Puck o' Pook's Hill*, the *Jungle Books* or the *Just So Stories*.

Students reading for the first time take the selection which the average number of their own contemporaries in age are reading.

All grades are carefully tabulated and posted up in a prominent place in the school, the reasons for the grade given are entered in the annual school report.

Registers of all grades are kept in alphabetical order and constantly consulted by the examiners.

The points for which marks are given are: pure vocal tone, vowel standard, clear articulation, intelligent phrasing and emphasis, actual artistic excellence and freedom in interpretation.

The work of a specialist teacher should be very largely co-ordinative. It is important, for instance, that only one definite method of respiratory training should be taught throughout the school. This method should be solely that suited to the development of good vocal tone. It should supersede in the physical training classes the useless complications of combined movement and breathing practice. If a sound method of breathing for voice has been established throughout the school, and is practised in the physical training class, in the singing and in the speech classes, that method will automatically adapt itself to all varying positions and movements without diverting attention to the effect of arm-raising or trunk-bending on the actual respiratory movement. All such diversion of attention tends to weaken automatic co-ordination, and often diminishes the actual chest expansion it is supposed to increase, or attains chest development at the expense of control. No test which can be applied by any but a qualified medical man, will compare for accuracy and certainty with the test of vocal tone in determining the quality and freedom of respiratory movement; it will detect defects which would never be felt in the practice of physical exercises, and ensure proper medical examination and treatment.

The confusion in the mind of a child who is being given one set of "breathing exercises" in drill, another in singing-class, and possibly another in recitation, or under the energetic guidance of a phonetic language teacher or a teacher of solo-singing, is easily imagined.

The standard of vowel sound in speech and song should be the same throughout the school. The distinction between the formation of vowel sound and the selection of the sounds used in individual words or in different languages, has been already described, but here it is important that the teacher should have a sufficient knowledge both of vocal and phonological method, and of phonetics. A large part of the confusion which exists in the teaching of spoken English arises from lack of ear-training, lack of practice in phonetic transcription, and ignorance of the nature of vowel resonances.

If such grading and training is carried out throughout the school, the teachers of ordinary English subjects will be relieved from a very great part of the necessity for endless nagging correction; they will find it better to make a note of any very constant or marked error, and pass it on to the teacher responsible for speech-training to overcome by steady and appropriate practice.

But it will still be necessary to insist on general clarity of articulation throughout the school. The teacher of mental arithmetic should no more accept "fits" and "sits" for fifths and sixths than he would accept ill-made figures in the working out of a sum. The mind works harmoniously; clarity of utterance helps clarity of thought.

Where it is not possible to obtain the help of a trained teacher of speech it must not be forgotten that in an English school, as the Departmental Committee on English pointed out in their report, every teacher can and should be a teacher of English.

Here the co-ordination suggested above can be carried out in a less certain manner, but still with useful results. The singing class should always begin with respiratory and vowel practice. The teacher of physical training should be sufficiently familiar with the needs of the voice, to avoid stiffening chests or sacrificing control to force. The teachers of English and of foreign languages should work out some common phonetic standard and try and tabulate their students' mistakes for mutual reference.

Till all training colleges place the acquisition of good English speech and of pure unforced vocal tone in the forefront of their curriculum, this will not be possible even in very fully staffed schools; but the growing sense of the importance of spoken English is an unquestioned fact, and before long a genuine standard may be achieved.

Some practical points may be of use to teachers who have not had special training in speech.

Where a strong local accent has to be combated, it will be found best always to begin by trying to secure pure vocal tone, and to establish the fundamental positions of the vowel scale.

This method avoids offending the strong patriotic attachment to provincialisms, and provides a reason for such corrections as are genuinely necessary. Variation in vowel use is comparatively unimportant; it is error in vowel quality and faulty vocal tone which offend the ear.

Insist that song and speech are one. The fundamental principles of speech formation must precede any attempt at formal teaching of singing.

Never attempt to enforce pedantic or class standards of speech in a haphazard manner during school hours. The only result is that the students become spasmodically bi-lingual. Interest each student in speech as a whole, give everyone a clear idea of the general level, good or bad, of their daily speech, and give every "C3" the eager desire to attain to an "A1" level.

Criticism, without clear analysis of the defect criticised and accurate instruction in a method of cure, is merely exasperating, and promotes self-consciousness.

If it be objected that the standard of English speech is still too vague to be critically enforced, it will, I think, be found that the objection is theoretical rather than practical.

We all know when a speaker is clearly audible without effort. We can all distinguish a round, clear spontaneous tone in the speaking voice from one which is harsh, irritating, or affected. We can all see whether the movements of speech are lightly, rhythmically and beautifully performed, or whether they are vague, exaggerated or inaccurate. Anyone can draw up a list of twenty ordinary vulgarisms of pronunciation and articulation which are inadmissible in educated speech. If these simple things are done first, the improvement in muscular and nervous control which will follow will soon be apparent, and vexed questions of "standard" or "modified standard" or "dialect" will soon fade into insignificance. In practice we all know good speech when we hear it. It is usually that good speech which seems, like Dogberry's reading and writing, to "come by nature," not to result from effortful and conscious control.

But, given proper opportunities, that speech and no less is the natural heritage of every citizen and should be assured to him. Incidentally nothing would more surely diminish the undue influence and attraction of cheap oratory than such a widely diffused standard of sound speech-training.

The defects referred to in this and the previous chapter may be tabulated as follows:

i. Lack of flexibility in inspiratory movement.

ii. Poor chest development, often resulting from nose or throat trouble.

iii. Lack of control and rhythm in expiratory movement, resulting in:

iv. Breathy tone.

v. Harsh attack or "shock."

vi. Nasal tone caused by weak palate-movement, or conversely by nasal obstruction which impedes true nasal resonance.

vii. Throaty tone due to narrowed throat passages, and weak respiratory force.

viii. Faulty vowel shapes; inaccurate use of subordinate vowels.

ix. Defective articulation, often due to defective dentition.

x. False stress, generally on prepositions, conjunctions and pronouns, due to scanned accents instead of rhythmic phrasing.

xi. Mechanical falling inflections at the close of every sentence or at the end of every line.

xii. Singsong inflection following the mechanical scansion of the line.

xiii. Colloquial delivery, exaggerating the sense-stress and destroying rhythm.

xiv. Meaningless variety in tone, stress and movement.

CHAPTER VII

THE STUDY OF PROSODY

WHEN we are dealing with students whose interest in literature is awakening we are often asked whether prosody is of any real use to them. Do we need to be able to scan verse?

From the point of view of this book the question becomes practically this: Do we or do we not speak verse differently when we definitely know its metrical basis?

I believe that we do. But before trying to demonstrate this, it would be well to think for a moment what we mean by "scansion," and what it is we are doing to verse when we "scan" it.

Most people in scanning verse tick off the syllables:

The qùa litỳ of mèr cy ìs not strài ned.

te tùm |te tùm |te tùm |te tùm |te tùm. |

What does this profess to represent? Certainly not the words as they are ever spoken. And with equal certainty not the metric scheme of the line, since it is a system of corresponding accent and quantity, all the accents being made into long periods, though they are spoken staccato without duration; really musically, like this:

The qual - i - ty   of mer - cy   is   not   strained.

It does not seem as if this exercise would be of much value to anyone.

If on the other hand we substitute musical notes for accents in the manner which has been advocated by William Thompson in his *Basis of English Rhythm*, we should get: [1]

The   quality | of mer-cy | is not | strained.

This is much more useful, for by this we could re-produce exactly the notation of the line. But is this again " scansion "? Surely not. It would serve equally well for:

" Do come with me |to church | next Sunday | morn - ing."

It is writing out the sentence-stress in its nearest equivalent of musical notes, and is applicable to prose as well as verse, while what we want is not the tune but the fundamental pulse-beat behind the tune.

To put it another way, it is treating rhythm as time. Now in music we do not *count* the number of notes in a bar, nor do we *play* the time-signature; we count the beat while we play the melody to it. So we ought neither to count the rhythm, nor the syllables, nor do we speak the metre—we should speak *to* it.

If we turn back to rhythm for a moment we find that in music we count an equal number of beats between any two accented notes, demanding that the spacial element of the melody shall exactly fill the intervening time, but indifferent through how many note-steps it passes on the way.

[1] *The Basis of English Rhythm.* Wm. Thomson. Glasgow, 1904.

Sterndale Bennett, "Barcarolle" Op. 19.
Bars 1 & 2.

Bar 24.

In verse do we not simply count the isochronous accents at regular intervals, and demand of the spacial movements of vowels and syllables that their duration shall fit in accurately into the intervals of the accents, never violating their own sentence - stress, duration, or significance?

So we hear a fundamental isochronous beat of accent, under the free flow of a speech rhythm. This would be the true scansion of verse. This would be Robert Bridges' "stress prosody" with one element added; a thread of regular durational value spacing the distances between the accents and helping to control, not indeed the quantity, but rather the tempo, quickness or slowness, of the intervening words, their relation in time to the principal accents.

I own this answer does not completely explain the whole musical impression of verse. I think it is as far as we can get at present; till English speech is spoken with much greater exactitude, or perhaps till poetry and music have become once more united by a greater freedom of time-structure in music, and less exaggerated accent in speech. What does this stress prosody help us to do? Pretty much, it seems to me, what counting in music helps us to do; it puts us right when we lose our instinctive rhythm.

The poet himself feels a verse tune just as a musician hears a melody, without stopping to count its allotted beats. Making it perhaps out of some succession of natural sounds, and, if we may judge by the notebooks of great musicians, often working it through two or three slightly different time-pulses before satisfying himself that he has determined the best fundamental pulse-beat notation for his music.

The knowledge of the metric structure, *i.e.* of the number of stresses and the system of syllables they carry, may then help to put us straight if we lose the instinctive rhythm-beat.

Read the following words without consciously trying to recompose their verse:

I ought to have done more: once my speech, and once your answer, and there the end, and Edith was henceforth out of reach! Why, men do more to deserve a friend, to be rid of a foe, get rich, grow wise, nor, folding their arms, stare fate in the face. Why better even have burst like a thief and borne you away to a rock for us two, in a moment's horror, *bright, bloody and brief*: then changed to myself again: "I slew myself in that moment! a ruffian lies somewhere: your slave, see, born in his place!"

ROBERT BROWNING, Too Late.

Notice particularly the words in italics. Then compare with Browning's printed text. But a simpler instance may be obtained from one of Calverley's delightful parodies:

In lone Glenartney's thickets lies crouched the lordly stag,
The dreaming terrier's tail forgets its customary wag;
And plodding ploughmen's weary steps insensibly grow
    quicker,
As broadening casements light them on toward home, or
    home-brewed liquor.

It is in brief the evening—that pure and pleasant time,
When stars break into splendour, and poets into rhyme;
When in the glass of Memory the forms of loved ones shine—
And when, of course, Miss Goodchild's is prominent in mine.

. . . . . .

And evermore when winter comes in his garb of snows,
And the returning schoolboy is told how fast he grows;
Shall I—with that soft hand in mine—enact ideal Lancers,
And dream I hear demure remarks, and make impassioned
answers.

CHARLES STUART CALVERLEY, *Visions.*

Impossible combinations of well-known lines are here
threaded together. In the last verse the rhythm falters
for a moment till one realises the parody of Macaulay's
Horatius, and then it swings absurdly into:

> And evermore when winter
> Comes in his garb of snows,
> And the returning schoolboy
> Is told how fast he grows.

Here the knowledge of the verse gives us the key to
the phrasing intended.

In the comparison of stress scansion with the older
tables of metrical feet the following tables will be
found of use:

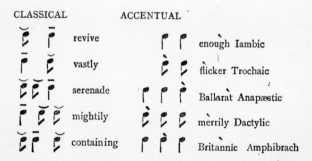

CLASSICAL			ACCENTUAL		
revive			enough Iambic		
vastly			flicker Trochaic		
serenade			Ballarat Anapæstic		
mightily			merrily Dactylic		
containing			Britannic Amphibrach		

No others are of any practical metric importance, but two are constantly referred to in older critical works on metre; these are the Pyrrhic and the Spondee:

pĭtў ⏑⏑   vīne - leaf ‾ ‾

These will be found in the course of certain metrical constructions, but in practice every English word has a slight accent, so they cannot be heard in single words. Accentually we say

pìtў   vìne-leaf

making them into trochees. We are also content with these accents:

shădōw) accentual   Trochee
pìllōw) quantitative Iambic.

The following suggestions for rules of rhythmic verse-speaking are based on the stress rules devised by Robert Bridges in his *Milton's Prosody*.[1]

(1) The stresses of English verse must recur at regular intervals in time, and these stresses must be in themselves speech stresses falling on words which are stressed in the sentence as it is naturally spoken.

Exception: A metric stress is admissible on the rhyme in closely rhymed verse such as couplets and quatrains.

Examples. False stress: (*a*)

> But shè was còy, and shè would nòt believe
> That hè did lòve her sò,
> No, nòt at *àny* tìme she woùld
> Any coùntenance *tò* him shèw.
> > *The Bailiff's Daughter of Islington.*

---

[1] *Milton's Prosody, with a Chapter on Accentual Verse, and Notes,* by Robert Bridges.

Rhyme stress in quatrains: (b)

> Thēy sày |thĕ Lìon |ănd thĕ Lìzārd |kèep |
> Thĕ Coùrts |whēre Jàmshĭd |glòriĕd |ănd drānk dèep. |
> E. FitzGerald, *Omar Khayyám*.

In the following examples stressed syllables are marked ` ;

Long unstressed ⁻;

Short unstressed ⌄;

Syllables prolonged by the voice ᵒ.

It is very important to acquire the power of hearing long unstressed syllables, and distinguishing them by duration from short syllables and by smoothness from stressed syllables.

(2) Each stress carries with it a certain number of syllables; not more than one heavy or two light on either side.

The stress will not carry a heavy syllable which is divided from it by a light syllable, and all stresses tend to hold together those syllables which have verbal or logical unity.

The following example from a well-known hymn worked out by Robert Bridges will illustrate this rule.

Scansion by counting syllables only:

> Brìghtest and |bèst of the |sòns of the |mòrning. |

Following the rule that a stress has most carrying power over the syllable next to it, we should get:

> Brìghtest |and bèst of |the sòns of |the mòrning. |

But as a stress has greatest attraction for verbal unity we arrive at:

> Brìghtest | and bèst | of the sòns | of the mòrning.

And this is the true scansion of the line.

(3) When four or more unstressed syllables occur

together the stress may be distributed over the four,
and the line will lack one of its stresses.
Example:

> Stĭckĭng tŏgĕthĕr | ĭn călămĭty.
> Stickìng | togèth | er | ìn | calà | mitў. (Scansion.)
> (*King John*, Act III. Scene 4.

(4) The first foot of a line preferably carries only one
syllable before the stress.

> Oh Yoùng | Lochinvàr | has come oùt | of the Wèst. |

(5) Any foot may be inverted.

1. *Inversion of the first foot:*

> Whàt ĭf hĕr eỳes wēre thère | thèy ĭn hĕr heàd.

2. *Second foot:*

> Dòst thōu lòve mĕ? | I knòw thŏu wìlt sāy " Aỳ."

3. *Third foot:*

> Bè nŏt hĕr màid, | sìnce shĕ ĭs ènviōus. |

4. *Fourth foot:*

> *See* Example 1 above.

5. *Fifth foot:*

> Àftĕr lōng seèmĭng deàd, | —Ĭàg[ŏ] hùrt hĭm.

(6) Where there is a grammatical pause in the line,
that pause determines the median break. Where there
is no such pause the verse balances into two parts,
with a pause, at, or near, the centre.

> Of one that loved not wisely,] but too well;
> Of one not easily jealous,] but, being wrought,
> Perplex'd in the extreme;] of one whose hand,
> Like the base Indian,] threw a pearl away
> Richer than all his tribe;] of one whose subdu'd eyes,
> Albeit unusèd] to the melting mood,
> Drop tears as fast] as the Arabian trees.
> Their medicinal gums.

(7) Poems in which the speech rhythms used are colloquial, follow grammatical and verbal unity closely, even breaking metric rules to maintain it. Poems, further removed from ordinary speech, or formal poems, maintain their exact metric structure even at the cost of grammatical unity. This last rule applies particularly to the treatment of overlapping lines.

These lines occur in two forms:

i. Lines in which the sense of the first is carried through the end verse-pause or rhyme and ends at some point in the second.

ii. Lines in which a sentence beginning in the last words of one line is completed in the second.

> (a) He ceased; and next him, Moloch, sceptered king,
> Stood up, the strongest and the fiercest spirit
> That fought in heaven, now fiercer by despair.
>
> MILTON, *Paradise Lost.*

> (b)   And I, who thought
> This Aziola was a tedious woman,
> Asked who is Aziola? How elate
> I felt to know that it was nothing human.
>
> SHELLEY, *The Aziola.*

There are six different ways of meeting the difficulty of the overlap.

1. In blank verse the lines may run continuously, a slight upward suspension of tone at the end of the first will link and yet distinguish the two without breaking the sense or obscuring the metric form.

> Sir, she's mortal;
> But by immortal Providence she's mine:
> I chose her when I could not ask my father
> For his advice, nor thought I had one.
>
> *The Tempest,* Act V. Scene i.

2. The same degree of overlapping in rhymed verse must be slightly held at the first rhyme:

That the lòwest boùghs and the brushwood shèaf
Round the èlm-tree bòle |are in tìny lèaf.
R. BROWNING, *Home Thoughts from Abroad*.

And why so quìetly go the great engines of my bòat
As if their sòuls were free.
FLECKER, *Santorin*.

In satyric verse or narrative the lines may run on:

With Farmer Allan at the farm abode
William and Dora. William was his son,
And she his niece.
TENNYSON, *Dora*.

3. The same effect is produced in so-called "free verse" by the introduction of a single long line:

Such delìght
As prìsoned bìrds must fìnd in frèedom,
Wìnging wìldly acròss the whìte
Òrchards and dàrk-green fièlds; òn, òn, and òut of sìght.
SIEGFRIED SASSOON, *Everyone Sang*.

(A series of a long wave-beats with no pause at the end of second line and no breath till "fields," then failing beats to "sight," gives the rhythm of this line.)

4. In the case of a very short overlap not reaching to the median pause of the second line, a compensating pause may make it possible to transpose a word to the second line:

You demi-puppets, | that
By moonshine do the green-sour ringlets make,
Whereof the ewe not bites;
The Tempest, Act V. Scene i.

N

Stress on the final word of the line will make
a slight end - pause possible in cases where
there is no sense - pause, and so transfer the
next word back to the first line: [1]

And yòu |whose pàstime—

Is |to make midnight mushrooms, that rejoice |

To hear the solemn curfew.

Ibid

6. Where the new sentence-period begins at the very
end of a line, it is often possible to avoid an
overlap by the change of voice needed for a
parenthesis:

Whereon

A treacherous army levied |one midnight
Fated to the purpose |did Antonio *open*
The gates of Milan;

The King,

His brother and yours, |abide all three distracted.

In sonnet-form overlapping is often very marked:

It keeps etèrnal whìsperings |aróund
Dèsolate shòres, |and with its mighty swèll
Glùts twìce tèn thòusand càverns, |till the spèll
Of Hècate |lèaves them their old shadowy soùnd.

KEATS.

If the swing of the lines is given freely the rhyme-
stress (2) will prevent any loss of verse-form.   Such
poetry as this must be held against undue sentence-
stress; the meaning will be clear unless the end of the
line is allowed to drop in pitch or a full verse-pause

[8] See Chapter III. for the full analysis of this passage.

introduced at the overlap; here no breath should be taken till after "shores."

In Rupert Brooke's *The Dead*, IV., a very beautiful change of rhythm is indicated by an overlap:

> There are wàters blown by changing wínds to laùghter |
> And lìt by the rich skìes all dày. || And àfter,
> Fròst, |with a gèsture, |stàys the waves that dánce
> And wàndering lòveliness. || He leaves a white
> Unbroken glòry, |a gathered ràdiance, |
> A wìdth, |a shining pèace, |under the nìght.

1914.

The poet's punctuation indicates the treatment of the rhyme-pause. In all these poems the same principle can be seen. When the speaker rises to the level of true poetic diction, the strangeness of the metric stress is part of that beauty, and must be maintained. It is at such a point that Shakespeare gathers together all the forces of the line, stress, duration, pitch, and emphasis, into unison:

> The cloùd-capp'd tòwers, the gòrgeous pàlaces,
> The sòlemn tèmples, ⅂ the great glòbe itsèlf,
> Yeà, àll which it inhèrit, shall dissòlve,
> And, lìke this ìnsubstàntial pàgeant fàded,
> Leàve not a wràck behìnd.

It is the music of which he alone has the secret.

In lyric verse, Keats achieves the same inevitable rhythm of sense and sound in:

> Chàrm'd màgic càsements, | òpening on the fòam
> Of pèrilous sèas, in fàery lànds forlòrn.

Each passage instantly breaking into a lightly stressed line which relieves the tension of the beat.

The same method is heard in one of the most perfect of all the sonnets; the dirge—

> No lònger moùrne for mè when I am déad,

breaking into the ironical fall of the close—

> Lèst thĕ wìse wòrld | shōūld loòk ĭntŏ yōūr mòan
> And *mock* yŏu wìth mĕ, ⅂ àftĕr I ăm gòne.

The effect of such momentary unison in all the
elements of rhythm is the greatest thing in poetry, but
we detest it if it becomes mechanical. If we hear a
speaker seeking constant identity between loud and
quick, or soft and slow, rising in loud or sinking in soft
passages, and making an inevitable connection between
one type of sentence and one type of inflection, all
music disappears and the performance reaches the
barrel-organ stage. Yet every speaker must take the
pains to read and identify the very best intonation and
emphasis he can discern in any passage, and be ready
to modify it directly he sees a better. Always remembering it is the principles only that are fixed, the
application must be individual. If the pauses indicated
in these examples are considered it will be found they
fall into four classes.

No speaker should ever be compelled to pause for
breath. In very rapid passages or in very long sustained
lines, breath should be taken quite imperceptibly as in
singing; it is for this that a very high degree of flexibility in breathing is required. But the trained speaker
can easily sustain for fifteen seconds, and no sentence
requires such an effort.

The opening lines of the *Morte d'Arthur* are an example
of a long hold which cannot be avoided:

> So all day long the noise of battle rolled
> Among the mountains by the winter sea;
> Until King Arthur's Table, man by man,
> Had fallen in Lyonnesse about their Lord,
> King Arthur.
>
> TENNYSON, *Idylls of the King.*

But there are enough pauses to make it quite easy if the tone is properly sustained.

In the opening lines of the "Good News from Ghent" the rapid pulse and tempo of the lines make it difficult to breathe fully, but it is possible to breathe at every strongly stressed final breath-consonant, *i.e.* in words like "stirrup," "gallop'd," "speed," "rest," and also, what is equally important, to allow some air to escape. It is a good rule always to take in a little air at every real sense-break whether it is needed or not.

There remain (√) metric pauses, final and median; or the pause marking the outline of stanzaic verse.

> From Harmony, √ from heavenly Harmony √
> This universal frame began; √
> When Nature underneath a heap √
> Of jarring atoms lay, √
> And could not heave her head. √
> The tuneful voice was heard from high, √
> Arise, √ ye more than dead.

If these pauses are vital to the metric structure they must be held for the value of a metric beat, *i.e.* for the value of a stressed or unstressed beat in the line in which they occur. Failure to do this, a system of hurried and audible breath-gasps which should be metric pauses, is perhaps the most usual fault of the nervous untrained verse-reader.

(2) The majority of metric pauses are sense-pauses. An example of a purely metric pause is found in line 3 of the last example; but not all sense-pauses are metric.

In lines from *The Tempest* on page 181, the "And" at the beginning of line 4—

> And, like this insubstantial . . .

cannot take a metric pause and it should if possible be

avoided: the comma is of course inserted by a later grammarian and not in the Folio.

(3) Where a sense-pause contradicts the metric pause, the same rule must be followed as in regard to overlap; the general level of diction required must be considered.[1]

(4) The speed of the whole poem is another factor which must be considered in relation to pause, and then in regard to the general metric effect of the whole rhythm.

This is perhaps the closest link between form and thought. The speed or, as it is called in music, the "tempo" of the poem is almost altogether governed by its subject-matter and the nature of its visual and auditive imagery. Looked at more carefully, I believe it will be found that nearly all the more beautiful instances of onomatopœia are the result of delicate adjustment of speed. Not the mechanical examples of Pope—

> Not so when the swift Camilla scours the plain,
> Flies o'er the unbending corn, and skims along the main,

but the way in which variation of speed will lighten or intensify stress and change the whole imagery of a poem as in Shelley's *Ode to the West Wind* or in two verses of the first chorus of *Atalanta in Calydon*.

> When the Hoùnds of Sprìng are on wìnter's tràces,
> The mòther of mònths in mèadow and plàin
> Fìlls the shàdows and wìndy plàces
> With lìsp of lèaves and rìpple of ràin;
>
> Whére shall we fìnd her, hŏw shall we sĭng to her,
> Fŏld our hånds round her knêes, and clĭng . . .

Compare also the three verses of Masefield's *Cargoes*, quoted on page 159.

[1] See page 178 (7).

Every lyric must be given its individual speed, and the factor of syllabic charge is an important one here. If the syllabic charge is very heavy the result of any attempt to speak too rapidly is always comic.[1] The absurd effect of patter songs is obtained in this way. It is in regard to variation of speed and pitch, that the widest divergence exists among those qualified to speak about the art of speaking or reading poetry. We must of course look first to the poets themselves for guidance, but they differ profoundly among themselves, and rarely read any but their own lyric verse. It will, however, be useful to discuss these differences a little more fully.

They all agree in reminding us that poetry is an end in itself, not a means of conveying information or of arguing about things; they urge us to give up the chatty argumentative tones which result from fixed mechanical inflections, and from the metric "up and down" delivery which so many carry on from childish days. This, and a sort of wailful self-pity, or a pious distress, are the chief faults which foreign speakers find with English diction. Many reciters chat their lyric verse in a tone which suggests that the skylark is being invited to renew a long-lost acquaintanceship with the speaker.

The controversy is no new one. It seems as if at regular intervals each method in turn had been carried to excess, then reaction had set in, and for a time the more intelligent artists of the day had followed a new method, with the result that it became popular, was imitated by less intelligent people, grew mechanical and so fell into disrepute. Shakespeare was an advocate of very natural speech with a warning against mouthing on the one hand and tameness on the other. Eighteenth-century Paris was torn in two by the controversy between Adrienne Lecouvreur and her rivals who still

[1] See page 140.

adopted a pseudo-classic chaunt. Among us the controversy is complicated by ignorance of English metric structure, loose use of technical terms and confusion between the two arts of dramatic and lyric speaking.

Here are a few of the points which the student is required to reconcile:

The ordinary reciter is apt to say, "Only feel what you are saying, and you are sure to express it properly." No one must undervalue the effect of simple and instinctive emotional power; but the result of this method is not infrequently an uneasy desire on the part of the audience to retire from an exhibition of emotion obviously of too private a nature for the general view.

The student of literature holds that understanding of the subject-matter and style of the poem is all that is required. But the speech of the average teacher of English is almost the least inspiring medium possible for the interpretation of poetry.

The poet asks us to give him "audible type"; any intrusion of the personality of the speaker will destroy the poet's meaning and music: "To add to his perfect expression this other feeble expression of our own is nothing but an impertinence." [1] To a great extent this view must be accepted. Gesture, deliberate use of facial expression, forced expression of any kind, destroys the whole intention of lyric verse; but three things must be remembered. First, the great difference between the visual impression of type, which we can go over and revive as often as we wish, and the infinitely more vivid but fleeting impression of audible words, which must be very perfectly arranged and stressed in time, if we are to retain their impression; and in which a single harsh or uncontrolled tone, or a pedantic or un-

[1] See above, page 157, Drinkwater's Introduction to *The Way of Poetry*.

usual or vulgar pronunciation, will at once spoil the
audible type, and reduce it to a poor and ill-made
scrawl. Secondly, unless the speaker or reader is perfectly in sympathy with, and full of understanding of
what he is reading, and *shows* this sympathy, the effect
will be one of boredom, and boredom soon communicates
itself from speaker to audience.

One thing more: the poet knows in his mind not only
the significance but the song of the verse. The ordinary
audience know nothing of this; and they are only
bewildered if a long-drawn, monotonous chaunt takes
the place of what they feel to be natural speech.

The speaker must find for English verse what the
French have already achieved for their more regular
and rhetorical line; a way of speaking which shall be
plain to the unlearned, yet inoffensive to those who
hate anything to come for a moment between them
and their silent memories of the verse they love.

Among the finest of our verse-speakers two poets
take widely different views of the art of verse-speaking.
One uses and teaches a regular rhythmic chaunt, which
effaces not only all the finer shades of metrical form,
but even any very clear sense of the words used or of
the sentence - structure. The range of such delivery
must remain too narrow. It can only be followed for
a very short time; its chief merit is to weave an atmosphere of dream within which the poet can work his own
magic. Hardly more than one form of poetry can be
so rendered, and the effect is so exotic and strange
that it leaves little memory of anything but that great
strangeness when the sound dies. And beside its strangeness, poetry, like all art, should transform and blend
life into unity and truth for us. It is dangerous to shut
out thought so completely from any art.

Another, perhaps the finest reader of lyric verse,

reminds us always that poetry is wrought out of words as statues out of stone; to him any sense of beauty in tone or voice is irrelevant, he hears only a verbal music. But surely the poet has more than words; he has a *dance* of words—images and music. Words are not always words, sometimes they are bonds and fetters from which we long to escape, and in poetry they fuse and glow white-hot into something beyond all words, into the life of rhythm which is the law of life itself.

It is little short of impertinence to criticise those who know so much of the true meaning of poetry, those indeed who have taught us more of the true art of speaking verse than any other teachers can accomplish; yet their very difference emboldens one. And, curiously, all have again and again agreed in pronouncing not far from excellence, readings by individual speakers very different from those they personally advocate in theory.

In practice the value of these theories is somewhat discounted by the fact that, as I have already said, their exponents generally read only their own verse, and firmly refuse to be beguiled into reading anything which does not immediately lend itself to their particular method. Therefore the following suggestions rather than criticisms may be ventured.

No method can be universally valid. Each form of poetry needs its own musical interpretation.

Given the capacity for perfect clarity, and rhythmic utterance, sense of style will be the surest guide in achieving a true interpretation, if it is combined with capacity for true emotional intensity; this will sustain the poem throughout at its right level, and so hold the attention of the audience.

Gesture is always annoying in lyric recitation, but in satyric it is often amusing and characteristic.

Dramatic verse is a thing quite apart and governed by

the rules of dramatic art as well as by the general
principles of metric delivery.

Personal methods influence us. The mental picture
or phantom of sound which serves as a standard within
the mind of each of us is based quite as much on the
muscular memory of speech-movement within the brain
as on the sound we hear during our own speech. We
feel, rather than hear, ourselves speak. We therefore
tend to like speech which is pretty much at our own
level of utterance. Even a stammerer will prefer to
stammer, rather than adopt a more vocal or forceful
delivery which would help him, while his obsession was
being conquered.

If you have to improve a person who speaks with
wide, motionless lips, and tightly closed jaws, a soft,
husky, toneless voice, and a face utterly without facial
movement, you will find it most difficult to persuade
him that you are not asking for the most exaggerated
sounds. Each of us is accustomed to associate the
mental content we wish to utter with just that degree
of force we ourselves employ in muscular action; if we
induce a student to use more than this he will feel that
he is being made most conspicuously ridiculous. Just as
a person who has moved in a false balance with badly
poised figure, bent knees and poking head will, on being
first persuaded to shift his balance, feel that he is
falling forward on his face.

The unemotional and constrained mentality which
is characteristic of such unforceful speech, at once
caused by it and confirming it through the habit of
repression, will dismiss as forced and unnatural the
simplest expression of æsthetic feeling; therefore poetic
appreciation needs to be cultivated by audible outward
flow of expression quite as much as by the inward flow
of silent appreciation.

CHAPTER VIII

DRAMATIC VERSE

To understand the function of dramatic verse, it is necessary first to consider its influence and effect in the theatre. Whatever may be the view held about the value of verse-speaking in the case of lyric or narrative poems, it must be recognised that dramatic verse is meant to be spoken. There is, I believe, no case on record where drama which has failed when brought to this supreme test has afterwards been recognised as of true literary merit. On the contrary, many works which claimed the admiration of their contemporaries as too fine, too poetic for representation on the stage, are seen in the judgment of a later day as rhetorical, ill-wrought and pretentious.

Dramatic poems, or plays in verse, may be more or less limited in their appeal, or they may suffer eclipse, as Shakespeare himself suffered it, during some passing aberration of fashion or taste; the recognition of a writer may be delayed because he requires for his plays greater scenic or mechanical resources than the contemporary theatre can afford him, but the great dramas of the world have been written with no other end in view than dramatic representation; if the poetic expression they employ is of such a character that it fails to move us when we hear it spoken with a sense of dramatic fitness, and with conviction, then the work is not in the true sense a play.

Of that which really moves us in the theatre there can be little question; it is the conflict of character

190

and circumstance. But as the painter must confine his creation to the space at his disposal on wall or canvas, so the dramatist must "stage" the conflict for us within the walls of his chosen theatre. He must reckon with the practical limitations of time, of space and of intensity which are conditioned by a hundred causes outside his art form. His theatre may be the temple of a divinity, the shrine of a faith, the arena of a circus, the meeting-place of a keenly critical and cultured group of people, the saloon of a prince, or the casual place of entertainment of a company of after-dinner smokers. He may be bounded by rules and conventions so strict, that inspiration seems almost incredible, or his patrons may be ready to excuse any eccentricity so long as they receive that thrill of laughter or surprise for which they have paid; whatever the conditions, he must work with them, and there accomplish the traffic of his play. He cannot merely describe his happenings, he must show us those he considers the most vital. He cannot explain his characters, they must come before us, speak and convince us of their reality. At one time, as in the Greek theatre or in the miracle play, he may take his plot from any half-dozen stories with which his audience are already familiar, and concentrate all his attention on the development of the emotion it suggests through beauty of poetical speech and subtle presentation of character. At another, as in melodrama or the Italian conventional comedy, he may select a set of conventional puppets whose whole range of typical action is known beforehand, and exert his ingenuity purely in fitting them into new and unexpected situations and settings. But he must interest us—either, if he is a dramatist, in the living creations of his brain, or, if he is a playwright only, in the clever capers he imposes on their woodenness.

It all has its place in that wonderful world of the theatre; a world to which we must not dare to set other limitations than those of its own devising, since from the father of tragedy himself, to the greatest of living "impersonators," all have found in it the expression of their own artistic inspiration, the means of delighting, inspiring, transporting their audiences.

Even when we limit ourselves to the consideration of drama in verse, the range of the subject is enormous; from the earliest tragedies to the latest patter song of the comedian; and each, if it is perfect of its kind, has a claim to rank among the things worth doing.

What is the place of poetry, in its true sense, in drama? It is obviously among those elements that give to drama its quality of idealism.

In its fundamental character, idealism never suggests unreality; the ideal grows within our mind from study of reality. When we say, "What a perfect rose," we mean that the flower we delight in meets within our mind the idea we had formed of all that most adorns a rose.

We never see the perfect flower, the perfect horse, the face of Golden Helen, yet we know if we did they would not be strange, but married to our thought. We should have little sense of their detailed perfection, only of the rest of perfect harmony. And we love all things the better because we hold in our heart the vision of their ideal reality.

So we have in our minds the ideal of perfect speech. Every lover hears himself in Romeo, every over-burdened soul speaks to us in Hamlet. They speak as we would have spoken, could we too have found words.

The appeal of dramatic poetry when it forms part of the art of the theatre, is as wide as its appeal in life.

It is used to give lyric beauty to passion, to give

points and delicacy to the merry banter of comedy, to give epic grandeur to a Lear or a Volumnia, but always it must speak through the lips of a human being, or it will become something different from drama. Very beautiful, possibly, in itself, but lacking harmony with character or circumstance.

It is always dangerous to suggest explanations or reasons for the greatness and for the undying fame of our Shakespeare. Each will find in him what he seeks. But it may, I think, fairly be suggested that his capacity for using poetry as an expression of character is one of the supreme secrets of his art. One instance may be given as proof of this: the failure of extracts to convey the slightest sense of the value and beauty of the passages selected. A good example is the often quoted "Quality of Mercy" speech from *The Merchant of Venice*. As a mere quotation it conveys no sense of its real significance in the play. It almost suggests a meaning directly opposed to that which it conveys there, and ends in a woeful anticlimax. The effect of having constantly studied and heard it, apart from its context, is to make it almost impossible to speak in the theatre, where it in no sense forms a "purple patch" for which actress and audience prepare themselves, with a deep inspiration of satisfaction at having reached well-known lines which can be let run along in a familiar cadence without dramatic relevance, as the "town-crier" might deliver it. The actress has to do her utmost to make us forget the recitation and remember the character and situation of Portia. Even more incredible is the case of the "Seven Ages." Here the music of the lines in their meditative flow has disguised the significance for those who know it only as an "elegant extract"; so that the cynical brutalities of Jaques, who sees loathsomeness alike in infant and grandsire, folly in love, self-interest in patriotism, conventional pedantry in the wisdom of experience—an attitude so foreign to Shakespeare's heart that he goes out of his way to denounce it in the person of the wise and kindly Duke as

> Most mischievous foul sin in chiding sin,

rounding his rebuke with words too forcible to quote—that these monstrous travesties of beauty and reverence are chosen as particularly suitable for children to learn by heart, and are constantly quoted as if they enshrined Shakespeare's own reasoned philosophy of life.

We should be readier to accept the claim of the teacher to be the true interpreter of Shakespeare's genius as opposed to the "frivolous and superficial" player, if he had not lent himself again and again to absurdities like this.

It is plain that the function of verse as Shakespeare uses it can only be maintained if the true rhythmic significance be audible throughout. To reduce it to the level of prose, as the actor so often does, is to sacrifice the essentially ideal effect intended by the poet, and so to diminish the extraordinary sense of transcendent significance which attaches to his characterisation. To deliver the verse as if it were lyric, with no sense that behind its cadences lies the music of actual speech, is to confirm a public delusion that plays in verse must be dull and unnatural.

Here it is above all important to insist on the matchless variety of Shakespeare's metric characterisation.

Mr. William Poel, whose intimate study of the whole question of Shakespearean performance, auditive as well as visual, makes him in this as in all such questions the one supreme authority, instances a case where the actual form of the verse, altogether apart from its meaning,

first drew his attention to the wrong attribution of a
passage. In *Hamlet*, Act V. Scene i.,

> This is mere madness:
> And thus awhile the fit will work on him;
> Anon, as patient as the female dove
> When that her golden couplets are disclos'd,
> His silence will sit drooping,

the First Folio and the First Quarto assign the lines
to the King. Mr. Poel, reading them so, was suddenly
arrested by the cadence of the lines as obviously spoken
by a woman. The Second Quarto verified the correction.

A short analysis of the elements needed for the
delivery of one only of the plays, *A Midsummer Night's
Dream*, may illustrate the mastery of variety which
Shakespeare requires from his actors. It contains:

i. *Sung lyrics often set or written to traditional tunes.*

  " Ye Spotted Snakes." " Through the House."

ii. *A parody of such folk-lyrics given to Bottom the
weaver.*

> The ousel cock so black of hue,
> With orange-tawny bill . . .

iii. *Lyric passage for the fairies, many in varied short
time metres.*

> Over hill, over dale,
> Thorough bush, thorough briar,
> Over park, over pale,
> Thorough flood, thorough fire.
>
> > Act II. Scene i.

> . . . . .
> Night and silence! Who is here?
> Weeds of Athens he doth wear:
> This is he, my master said,
> Despisèd the Athenian maid.
>
> > Act II. Scene ii.

o

iv. *Lyric passages for the lovers.*

Lys. Ay me! for aught that I could ever read,
  Could ever hear by tale or history,
  The course of true love never did run smooth;
  But, either it was different in blood;—
Her. O cross! too high to be enthrall'd to low!
Lys. Or else misgraffèd in respect of years;—
Her. O spite! too old to be engaged to young.
Lys. Or else it stood upon the choice of friends;—
Her. O hell! to choose love by another's eyes. . . .

   .   .   .   .

I swear to thee, by Cupid's strongest bow;
By his best arrow with the golden head;
By the simplicity of Venus' doves;
By that which knitteth souls and prospers loves;
And by that fire which burn'd the Carthage queen;
When the false Troyan under fire was seen;
By all the vows that ever men have broke—
In number more than ever women spoke—
In that same place thou hast appointed me,
To-morrow truly will I meet with thee.

Act I. Scene i.

v. *Parody of such verse and of contemporary dramatic
   writing in the Pyramus and Thisbe scenes.*

Pyr. I see a voice! now will I to the chink,
  To spy an I can hear my Thisbe's face.
  Thisbe!
This.   My love! thou art my love, I think.
Pyr. Think what thou wilt, I am thy lover still,
  And like Limander am I trusty still.
This. And I like Helen till the fates me kill.
Pyr. Not Shafalus to Procrus was so true.
This. As Shafalus to Procrus I to you.

   .   .   .   .

Pyr. Wilt thou at Ninny's tomb meet me straightway?
This. 'Tide life, 'tide death, I come without delay.

vi. *Rhymed heroic verse for Oberon and Titania.*

But we are spirits of another sort.
I with the morning's love have oft made sport;
And like a forester the groves may tread
Even till the eastern gate, all fiery-red,
Opening on Neptune with fair blessèd beams,
Turns into yellow gold his salt green streams.

Act III. Scene ii.

vii. *Shakespearean blank verse dialogue, sometimes with
   a large proportion of couplets.*

Eg. Happy be Theseus, our renowned Duke.
Th. Thanks, good Egeus: what's the news with thee?
Eg. Full of vexation come I, with complaint
   Against my child, my daughter Hermia.

Act I. Scene i.

Lys. Fair love, you faint with wandering in the woods;
   And, to speak troth, I have forgot our way:
We'll rest us, Hermia, if you think it good,
   And tarry for the comfort of the day.
Her. Be it so, Lysander: find you out a bed,
   For I upon this bank will rest my head.

Act II. Scene ii.

viii. *Blank verse with the roll of the great Shakespearean
   line, as perfect as any in the later plays.*

Hyp. I was with Hercules and Cadmus once,
   When in a wood of Crete they bay'd the bear, etc.

Act IV. Scene iv.

The. The poet's eye, in a fine frenzy rolling,
   Doth glance from heaven to earth, from earth to heaven,
And, as imagination bodies forth
   The forms of things unknown, the poet's pen
Turns them to shapes, and gives to airy nothing
   A local habitation and a name.

Act V. Scene i.

ix. *Ordinary folk-talk between the craftsmen in the contemporary speech of the day, quite probably suggesting his own Warwickshire neighbours' speech.*

Bot. First, good Peter Quince, say what the play treats on; then read the names of the actors, and so grow to a point.

. . . .

Yet my chief humour is for a tyrant: I could play Ercles rarely, or a part to tear a cat in, to make all split.

Act I. Scene ii.

x. *Prose lines for the Duke and his courtiers in Act V., used to help the ear in distinguishing the different speakers without losing the sense of absolute reality in the action of the mock tragedy.*

The. This is the greatest error of all the rest! The man should be put into the lantern, how is it else the man in the moon?

Dem. He dares not come there for the candle: for, you see, it is already in snuff.

Hip. I am aweary of this moon: would he would change!

The. It appears, by his small light of discretion, that he is in the wane: but yet, in courtesy, in all reason, we must stay the time.

Lys. Proceed, moon.

Act V. Scene i.

xi. *In addition we have the indication, as in* The Tempest *and many other plays, that certain passages were to be spoken to music.*

Obe. Silence awhile. Robin, take off this head.—
Titania, music call; and strike more dead
Than common sleep of all these five the sense.

Tita. Music ho! music; such as charmeth sleep.

Puck. Now, when thou wak'st, with thine own fool's eyes peep.

Obe. Sound, music. Come, my queen, take hands with me,
And rock the ground whereon these sleepers be.

Act IV. Scene i.

In this, one of the earliest of his original plays, we see Shakespeare experimenting in variety. In *Love's Labour's Lost*, a contemporary work, and a comedy of manners, we have an equal variety of diction. We have the parody there of the society smart talk of the day, that "euphuism" which was just going out of fashion among the fine gentlemen and ladies of the court. We have the pedantry of the growing race of "bookmen" with its laboured Latinity, its interest in the printed, as distinct from the spoken word, and its dry-as-dust scholarship at which Shakespeare for ever mocks, till in *Troilus and Cressida* he tilts against the whole spirit and tradition underlying it, the spirit from which he helped to save England.

Anyone who wishes to understand the part played by the actual diction of the plays in Shakespearean representation should study these two plays with special care, and above all William Poel's masterly analysis of the second, and of the controversy in which it played so decisive a part.

Let us now consider for a moment the exact object achieved by the eleven levels indicated in the *Dream*. One of the chief difficulties in the Elizabethan theatre was to obtain clear distinction between the different speakers as they came on or took up their parts in the dialogue.

On the stage itself, actors and a privileged few of the spectators were actually mixed together. The stage projected into the audience so that some part of it saw the performers from a side, or almost from a back, view only. When the players withdrew into the shadow of the "heaven," their faces could never have been very clearly visible; the actors of the day overcame their difficulties in a measure by the use of formal dumb-shows and by exaggerated facial expression, devices which Shakespeare disliked and ridiculed.

At no time was the personality of the individual actor "silhouetted," as on the modern stage, against a definite background by means of planes of lighting. He was left to make his own place chiefly by speech, in surroundings where range of dramatic action was much more limited than on the modern stage.

Costume, while it was rich and elaborate, was not, as in the theatre of to-day, made the chief vehicle for establishing sense of period, or personal atmosphere. Though, on the other hand, it is obvious that the use of contemporary costume does tend to make the audience intensely critical of the truth and sincerity of the players' acting. To convince an audience of regal dignity when dressed exactly like a contemporary monarch must have been a far harder task for a Cæsar in the "Globe" in 1603, than for a betogaed leading man in the reign of George V., with the aid of a thousand picturesque surroundings to confuse the critical instincts of his hearers.

Information contained in playbills, programmes, advance notices, etc., had to be given by word of mouth or by visible action to the Elizabethan audience. A great part of that audience, and the least lettered part, was standing, and therefore easily made restless. It was a very mixed audience, at every level of culture and intelligence, not, as in Molière's day, a specially chosen public under the discipline of court etiquette. For this theatre and audience Shakespeare wrote: not, it must be remembered, as a poet accomplishing his work and trying to get it accepted by some man of the theatre and adapted or revised for performance; not —after the very first period of his life in London—as a mere literary hack; not as a scholar indifferent to the dramatic fate of his work, but as a great poet who used for his medium the whole art of the stage, in which and on which he worked.

He often knew the smallest personal peculiarities, the
very intonations of the players for whom he was writing;
he always reckoned with his audience, even though he
set the censure of the one "judicious" above a whole
theatre of others. He considered the mechanical difficulties of his theatre and took advantage of its necessary
conventions in every scene he wrote; himself probably
a repressed rather than an emotional actor, he valued
intensity of expressive power in the highest degree,
and recognised how it could transform and inspire a
mediocre text, beyond the logical capacity of the player
who possessed it:

> This player here,
> But in a fiction, in a dream of passion,
> Could force his soul so to his own conceit
> That, from her working, all his visage wann'd;
> Tears in his eyes, distraction in's aspect,
> A broken voice, and his whole function suiting
> With forms to his conceit. And all for nothing!
> For Hecuba!
> What's Hecuba to him, or he to Hecuba,
> That he should weep for her?
>
> *Hamlet*, Act II. Scene ii.

No finer description of sheer emotional acting could
be given.

Of the applied arts of the theatre actually at his
disposal, he made greatest use of music. The mere
songs of the plays, without other work, would have
sufficed to assure the reputation of the greatest of our
purely lyric poets; and here again he distinguishes
between the use of words and music already familiar
to his audiences, to which he constantly refers, as in
Twelfth Night—lyrics set to new or traditional airs, part-
songs and madrigals—and passages where the magic
atmosphere of faery, of "soft stillness and the night,"
or of lovers meeting, is woven for us by some delicate

lutanist or well-played " chest of viols." Knowledge of music, the art of reading music, and the difficult art of speaking to, or above, music, is among the equipment Shakespeare expects of his interpreters. He probably found it pretty universally in his own day. How lamentably it fails him to-day, practically every Shakespearean performance ever given in a London theatre might illustrate. One instance is fresh in my mind: the sudden stopping of Oberon's most beautiful and most characteristic lines:

> I know a bank whereon the wild thyme blows, etc.,

while the orchestra took up the cue, and an extraneous fairy from the wings warbled an impertinent setting which distorts Shakespeare's words to fit its sing-song.

The kind of singing needed for this dramatic music is that to which special reference is made in the last chapter of this book, where words and music blend without effort and all operatic exaggeration is avoided.

Speaking to music as in the lines quoted above is a distinct and difficult art. The musical rhythm, being the more stable of the two, must be maintained, and the actor must speak to music, not speak followed by music. But as, in singing, the accompanist follows the voice without losing the shape of the accompaniment, so in "melodrame" the words must remain significant and linked by their logical and verbal unity. Perhaps the most perfect instance in Shakespeare is the restoration of Hermione in the *Winter's Tale*:

> Music awake her; strike!
> 'Tis tìme; |descènd; |be stòne no mòre: |approàch;
> Strìke all that loòk upon |with màrvel. | Còme; |
> Ì'll fill your gràve up: |stìr; |nay come awày;
> Bequeath to deàth your nùmbness, for from hìm
> Dear lìfe redeèms you, etc.
>
> Act V. Scene iii.

Here the words are written to music; very likely to that of harps or of a small organ. The short phrases each follow chords in rising intensity. Paulina is hardly thinking of what she says, only of bridging over the beautiful and terrible moment of reunion and recognition for husband and wife, the moment for which she has waited for sixteen years, fighting the intrigues of the courtiers anxious for the king's remarriage and the safety of the succession. Her words, the spell of the music, the measured rhythm of the queen's movement to it, hold back the angry protests of the doubting courtiers, the discomfort of Polixenes, the overwhelming emotion of the two chief actors, till that moment when the king's fingers close on living flesh and the cry of passionate assurance breaks through the measure of movement and words:

> Oh, she is warm!
> If this be magic, let it be an art
> Lawful as eating.
>
> Act V. Scene iii.

In words spoken to music, above all, Shakespeare would have us

> Suit the action to the word,
> The word to the action.

In Oberon's lines,

> Come, my queen, take hands with me, etc.,
> Act IV. Scene i.,

the music of the lines gives the rhythm of the stately movement needed, and changes later on for the tiptoe mischief of Puck's brief entrance and exit, and then to the growing climax of the hurried flight of the king and queen, so vividly heard that we should be able to picture them winging off into space to follow "the triple Hecate's team."

The crisp median pause, and stressed end-rhyme, which distinguish the fairy speeches illustrated in sections iii. and vi., again suggest the swift, decisive, single-minded action needed for the two great fairies, who never speak the language of their followers, nor that of the mortals among whom they move, invisible. They are spirits, things of fire and dew. It would be worth a great producer's time to spend hours in differentiating the speed, weight, and cadence of these lines from everything else that is spoken in the play; the absence of any dual thought or interest; the instant change of mood, the way in which the words avoid the chime and cadence of common speech; teaching the actors to efface all traces of intrusive human personality which would make the scenes between Titania and Bottom vulgar and repulsive. The quality of tone and diction needed is, of course, that of a young boy; such as we hear in the singing of a perfectly trained chorister's voice. In the speech of Puck and the fairies we are reminded of those

> demi-puppets that
> By moonshine do the green sour ringlets make
> Whereof the ewe not bites.

Words and movements have the quaint, jerked cadences of marionettes. One would like to see an experimental performance by those dainty dancers of Italy whose quaint wooden faces are best suited to the fixed mood of Puck's mischief.

> For those things do best please me
> That befall preposterously.

But his epilogue, with the poet's proud humility ringing

through it, needs more serious speaking and self-forget-
fulness than anything in the play.

One passage which needs special notice is Puck's
stage-direction speech in Act III. Scene ii., describing
in minutest detail a scene already played before us in
Act III. Scene i.

If, as is most likely, the play was originally a wedding
masque rather than a play, this may be due to some
peculiarity in the position of the audience making it
difficult for them to see clearly what had happened in
the first scene. Or it may be an instance of Shakespeare's
distrust of action as distinguished from speech. A distrust which makes him constantly tell the audience
what they should see. A method which an age like
the present, so markedly visual rather than auditive,
finds it difficult to understand.

Not long since, a prominent manager explained to
me why an audience could not be expected to care for
a performance of a poetic play during a series of ordinary
Shakespearean performances. This play being given
with the object of interpreting the poetry and character
rather than the scenery and " business " which could
be derived from it.

"You see," he said, "when they can go to the same
theatre any night and *see* a play acted, you can't
expect them to go just to hear the unimportant part—
the words—can you?"

I may say again that I believe the pictorial nature
of modern production, due almost entirely to scientific
discoveries in lighting, is responsible for our great
change of taste in this matter, a change leading to the
dislike of asides, soliloquies, and all that suggests a
fixed convention for stage traffic, apart from the accepted
convention of realistic illusion.

Of course this is the most complete convention of all;

for the illusion must never be binding. If it were, the audience would rush on the stage and pinion Macbeth as he goes out to murder Duncan.

The delivery of such a speech as this of Puck's (Act III. Scene ii.) must be a whirlwind "tour de force." We must take delight in the rapid mischievous recapitulation of what we already know, as we take delight in hearing for the hundredth time the clever patter of a song; it needs speed, clarity, and that intensity of projection which by itself excites and thrills like brilliant colour or vivid light.

This was the art of the Italian *buffo* singers and of the *commedia dell' arte*. It still survives in the conventional characters of the French theatre. We have put in its place, in movement, its equivalent in action: the run-about farce, or the knock-about comedian. We could probably still enjoy it in speech as we undoubtedly enjoy it in song, if we trained our players to do it as part of their natural technical equipment ; and if it came to them with perfect ease as one of the natural resources of their art. Where it is taught to a mature artist for a special occasion, it is usually inaudible, and sounds forced and hurried, while the audience begins wondering why the actor is hurrying so, and loses the thread of what is being said. Shakespeare's ordinary blank-verse dialogue is practically fool-proof. I have already discussed at length the nature of the compromise he established between the various metric elements and the cadences and stresses of ordinary speech.

He accomplished his task so perfectly by the gift, apparently, of an ear so super-sensitive, and with so tremendous a reserve of poetic force at his command for every climax and situation, that whether we concentrate on his meaning or on his music we can achieve almost equally good results.

A mere sense of metrical cadence will often enable a child to deliver a speech he can barely be expected to understand, with almost the perfection of a trained actor. On the other hand actors who can barely distinguish prose from verse, will often give the varied effect of his lines with perfect metrical taste simply by concentrating on the meaning, characterisation, and dramatic effect.

I am yet of opinion that if a true training in the art of verse-speaking, and above all of Shakespearean speaking, were a part, and an important part, of every child's education we should get three things:

(1) A better ensemble in the speech of all concerned in a big production.

(2) A keener critical sense and understanding in the audience of what is being done on the stage.

(3) A demand for a higher and better standard of production, less dependent on the accidents and more concerned with the essentials of Shakespeare's art.

Two other instances of the use of poetry in the theatre remain to be considered.—The various short plays where music, poetry, and scenic design are used to give an effect of fanciful and delicate unreality. The most perfect example of this is *Prunella*. Its performance needed, above all, the art of speaking to music with perfect variety and freedom, both by single characters, and in unison from groups of characters forming a spoken chorus. The genius of a great producer and of a charming musician, and the eager industry of a group of brilliant young actors, resulted in a performance which achieved something very like perfection and almost created a new art.

Many imitations, more or less successful, have

---

[1] *Prunella, or Love in a Dutch Garden*. Laurence Housman and Granville Barker.

followed, but nothing that has equalled the original. The diction required days of practice to get identity of cadence between the spoken phrase and the music, without chaunting or breaking the sense-rhythms.

Whenever such an experiment has been made with adequate study and rehearsal it has resulted in a great popular success. The work required is not beyond the reach of anyone who has had some training in music and song. The words must be taught from the beginning by someone who is completely familiar with the music. The music must be written to spoken words, and must follow the natural cadences of the speaking voice. At a sufficient number of points or resolutions the note of speech and of the music must harmonise, without destroying the sense-inflections.

As soon as possible, the speaker must go away from the instrument and music, and speak freely, till the two threads seem to run on independently and twine together as if each were woven into the other. If the music is orchestral it will need several full rehearsals, for the timbre of certain instruments, particularly that of the 'cello, the clarionet, and the oboe, is so near to the quality of the speaking voice that they drown it very easily—and in this case the instruments should be below or behind the speaker, if he is to be audible.

The last and, in some ways, the most interesting experiment, is that made by modern poets, who deliberately reject all ordinary dramatic effects and give us a pure lyric tragedy, which is best described in the preface to Yeats' *Plays for an Irish Theatre*:

It was only by watching my own plays that I came to understand that this reverie, this twilight between sleep and waking, this bout of fencing, alike on the stage and in the mind, between man and phantom, this perilous path as on the edge of a sword, is the condition of tragic pleasure, and to understand why it is so rare and so brief. If an actor becomes over-emphatic, picking out what he believes to be the important words with violence, and running up and down the scale, or if he stresses his lines in wrong places, or even if an electric lamp that should have cast but a reflected light from sky or sea, shows from behind the post of a door, I discover at once the proud fragility of dreams.

At first I was driven into teaching too statuesque a pose, too monotonous a delivery, that I might not put "vitality" in the place of the sleep-walking of passion, and for the rest became a little deaf and blind.

But alas! it is often my own words that break the dream. Then I take the play from the stage and write it over again, perhaps many times. At first I always believed it must be something in the management of events, in all that is the same in prose or verse, that was wrong, but after I had reconstructed a scene with the messenger in *Deirdre* in many ways, I discovered that my language must keep at all times a certain even richness. I had used "traitor," "sword," "suborned," words of a too traditional usage, without plunging them into personal thought and metaphor, and I had forgotten in a moment of melodrama that tragic drama must be carved out of speech as a statue is out of stone.

But train our players and mechanists as we will, and if we have not thought out the art of stage decoration afresh every brush-stroke of our scene-painter will mix into the reverie the meretricious or the irrelevant. We shall have hired some journeyman to accompany the poet's description with a painted landscape which, because it must give all to the first glance and yet copy nature, will alone copy what is obvious, and which even if it could keep the attention and give it pleasure could but keep it to the poet's loss.

YEATS' Preface to Plays for an Irish Theatre
(Shakespeare Head Press).

The earlier plays of Maeterlinck and Synge belong to this tradition. They escaped the danger which lies in wait for all English verse-drama : the overpowering force of the Shakespearean tradition; beautiful and penetrating as they are, they do, nevertheless, illustrate a dangerous tendency. They grow rhetorical. The monotone delivery required by the Irish producers is beautiful only for a very brief time, and under conditions of perfect and artistic simplicity.

Are these methods really of the theatre? Characterisation must be reduced to a minimum, circumstance is too inexorably limited. Many to whom they appeal beyond all other forms of dramatic art will be inclined to answer, "If not, so much the worse for the theatre"; but rhetorical drama has a disturbing history. It is true these things stand far from the arid period of Seneca; indeed, the delight they give is too fragile and almost too exquisite to endure. But at least they may claim to have restored a great simplicity and dignity to the art of acting, and to have added new chords to the instrument of the human voice.

Many modern prose plays need for their true delivery the qualities of poetic speech. The association of verse-speaking with the bombast of old "elocutionary" methods has left us without a tradition for such work. The horror of any speech-training whatever, which is openly expressed by nearly all our greatest actors and producers, is a result of the bad old methods. As an example of the results to be aimed at, one may instance the longer speeches of Bernard Shaw's plays, especially the last act of *Major Barbara*, and of *Heartbreak House*. Those who have spoken best in these plays have nearly all been trained in some measure of metric diction, but we need to purge our dramatic verse-speaking of every trace of artifice and unreality before we can serve the needs of the contemporary stage as they should be served in this respect.

CHAPTER IX

SATYRIC VERSE

It must be apparent to anyone reading the general account of poetic form in Chapter IV., that any hard and fast rules dividing the great poetic forms, and, more especially, definitions limiting English lyric poetry, are difficult to maintain.

Where should we place Browning's *Dramatic Romances*? Byron's *Childe Harold*? Shelley's *Queen Mab* or Keats' *Endymion*?

It is also clear that a very large category of true poetry, and all that is more commonly called verse, stands outside the scope of the three great forms.

Narrative poetry, didactic verse, occasional verse, comic verse, parody, burlesque,—the list recalls Polonius' exposition of the Players' repertory. It is with the intention of giving more precision to the definite divisions and finding more justification for certain critical rejections and inclusions that the term "satyric verse" has come to be used.

To the Greeks a satyric play meant primarily a work in which the accidents, and not the essentials, of poetry were stressed. Or, from another point of view, a play in which the action was allowed to dominate the true form of tragedy. The *Alkestis* was a satyric play because its central idea was too composite for tragedy; because passing circumstance and accident played a greater part in it than over-ruling fate. Because the centre of interest shifted from Alkestis to Admetos, and from Admetos again to Herakles; because Herakles became mildly intoxicated, because characters of lower rank—

P

a slave woman, a steward, and a child—brought pathos, or fleeting and personal emotion, into the action instead of the ethos, the heroic devotion of the wife who died for her lord. The play had in addition a happy ending outside the true logic of its circumstances, an accidental thing without bearing on the principle of the play.

Lack of proportion between content and force—the true harmony of poetry—and transient or topical interest, were included in the idea of a satyric drama; or the formal mocking of serious things which we call burlesque or parody.

The same conception seems valid for satyric verse to-day. It would include, first, formal verse, where form is the only object; and its opposite—neglect of form for some slight and topical preoccupation with subject-matter only. Among the first would rank the rondeau, the villanelle and other formal poems; the second gives us the pleasant little anecdote in verse, or even the words of a "drawing-room ballad." When these things are beautifully done, they attain to the level of satyric verse; when they fail they relapse into doggerel.

The parody, where form is impeccably preserved, but inharmoniously used for a trivial, ridiculous or incongruous content, is the most purely formal of all verse, and finds a place in this category.

Poetry limited by topical interest, or dated by the fashion of a period, is among the most beautiful of satyric poetry.

Pope's *Rape of the Lock* whose "merum sal" has acted as a preservative for over two hundred years; or Austin Dobson's exquisite reincarnation of the eighteenth century and the

> Glorious days of the Hanover line,

are perfect examples.

All verse which has too narrow a national character, or that verse-journalism which is inspired, however passionately, by passing accidents and dies

In the cradle where it lies.

It is in regard to writing of this kind that the test of time is above all essential. Such poetry, when it survives, survives through perfection of form, intensity of feeling, felicity of phrase, or through those elements of lyric richness and simplicity which lift it into essential beauty.

The definition may probably be held to include comic poetry—the smallest class of all—even the smallest class of good verse, apart from poetry, for there is very little which conveys to us that excitement and delight which must inform all except purely reflective rhythmic writing.

In English, since Chaucer's incomparable tales, there is nothing supremely great in this mode; on the lighter level, *John Gilpin's Ride*, the elegies *On a Mad Dog*, and *Madame Blaize*, a little Thackeray, perhaps one or two of the *Bab Ballads*, Browning's delightful *Pied Piper*—verbally rather than genuinely humorous—a few of Kipling's soldier songs, De la Mare's *Off the Ground*, Harvey's *Ducks*—too charged with sympathy for true comedy—these are all that one can quote. Calverley and Lewis Carroll should perhaps rank among the parodists.

Is this because the spirit of comedy is the latest growth of time, or because, as Yeats writes,

Tragedy must always be a drowning and breaking of the dykes that separate man from man, and that it is upon these dykes comedy keeps house?

Does comedy then demand the two fundamental elements of drama—character and circumstance—so that the only great comic poetry from Aristophanes to Molière must be in dramatic form?

Yet the great novelists, from Fielding to Meredith and Hardy, show us that the profound ironies of life can be interpreted through comedy as perfectly as in tragedy, and in one instance Byron's profound egoism alone seems to stand between him and that supreme achievement of satyric art. In considering the work of our moderns, some such development is not improbable. Light verse, rhymed plays, experiments in metric form, and a true art of music, colour and poetry in the theatre, are among the signs of the times; and for such work there is a demand which may create abundant response.

We have not yet purged our laughter of all cruelty, or of all senility, and it is true that comedy in lyric verse does tend to rest on that element of laughter which is superficial, and depends on the sense of incongruity; therefore it dies with the external circumstances that created it; for congruity is much a matter of fashion, and soon changes; we could not submit as we do to the vagaries of the passing mode, in all external things, if custom did not rapidly blunt our perception of incongruity.

Such a sense in its fundamental form inspires Shakespeare's glorious abusive metaphors, and makes Falstaff the touchstone of his genius, while without it Shelley lost his temper and soiled his pages over the fat hero of his later day, who claimed rank as the First Gentleman in Europe.

Satire is again a form of satyric verse, though the range of the two is not conterminous, but how little of it survives! *The Dunciad* is duller than the dolts it pilloried; Byron rants at his enemies like an ill-bred actor, Tennyson's second thoughts injure our appreciation of his earlier inspiration. In one form alone—the epigram—it has proved immortal. Its brevity, the point and finish of its form, enable it to triumph over the limited range of its subjects. Like the sonnet, it must touch but one point and exhaust that utterly. Nor need it always be satirical—witness Landor or Belloc:

> I strove with none, for none was worth my strife.
> Nature I loved, and next to Nature, Art:
> I warm'd both hands before the fire of life;
> It sinks, and I am ready to depart.
> WALTER SAVAGE LANDOR, *Finis.*

> Lady, when your lovely head
> Droops to sink among the Dead,
> And the quiet places keep
> You that so divinely sleep:
> Then the Dead shall blessed be
> With a new solemnity.
> For such Beauty, so descending,
> Pledges them that Death is ending.
> Sleep your fill:—But when you wake
> Dawn shall over Lethe break.
> H. BELLOC, *Dawn shall over Lethe break.*

There is no form of verse which gains more from the art of diction than the lighter forms of satyric verse; such work is the true French "art de dire," the most exquisite social and artistic charm, full of an aptness, delicacy, and distinction which has little parallel in England. It has been brought to perfection by great artists like Coquelin and Yvette Guilbert.

All the qualities which are out of place in lyric expression—personality, individual peculiarity, whimsical variety, and that strange quality which the actor calls "punch," which may be defined as the power of projecting oneself into the very hearts of an audience—all these have their true place here. The artist plays himself, not any other character; or travesties himself i n assuming another character. We have magnificent examples of the popular vein of this art in our music-hall performances, with their incomparable technical skill. Here the artist speaks straight at the public, and waits for his response. Just recently a few of our great actors have spoken lyric under these music-hall conditions, with astonishing results. If our poets could learn the technique of such writing, here is the greatest audience in the world ready to their hand. It is not an easy medium, for, to be speakable, poetry must possess the Shakespearean quality of giving perfect verse-form to uninverted and significant speech.

Among the qualities which the speaking or vocalising of satyric verse requires is a crystal clarity of articulation. It has been said that if the voice of tragedy is golden, that of comedy should be of silver. Next to this requirement one would place variety of resource in expression. For it is the unexpected that strikes home. Pointed emphasis, so disastrous in lyric verse, is irresistible in satyric, and that mischievous stressing of a clever rhyme, or an absurd rhyme, which was a genuine joy in the older burlesque. Pace, again; and the sense of rapidity in climax, which carries an audience away into a contagion of laughter or tears. Above all, its greatest charm is that it is so completely individual; a definite gift which cannot be acquired. This often blinds those who possess it to the no less important fact that no art is so merciless in its demands on technique. Complete physical mastery of bearing, speech, style, and personality must be achieved. It may be, and often is, an instinctive rather than a conscious technique, but in working with some of its greatest exponents, the conclusion becomes inevitable that nothing else requires quite such unfaltering hard work. For originality here is achieved only by the most extraordinary recombining of things personally experienced. Many of those who have excelled have been authors as well as performers in their programmes, and in many cases their work has proved a preparation for pure comedy later on.

The extraordinarily sharp characterisation required is almost like that of the silhouette cutter, whose little black figure, snipped while you wait, seems more like you than the costly triumphs of the fashionable photographer. How delicate the art might be on a smaller stage one can imagine from such little scenes as those which Austin Dobson made for his *Proverbs in Porcelain*—the fable of the jealous ladies from "The Cap that Fits," for instance:

> Myrtilla (lest a Scandal rise
> The Lady's Name I thus disguise,)
> Dying of Ennui, once decided,—
> Much on Resource herself she prided—
> To choose a Hat. Forthwith she flies
> On that momentous Enterprise.
> Whether to Petit or Legros,
> I know not; only this I know;—
> Head-dresses then, of any Fashion,
> Bore names of Quality or Passion.
> Myrtilla tried them, almost all:
> "Prudence," she felt, was somewhat small;
> "Retirement" seemed the Eyes to hide;
> "Content" at once was cast aside.
> "Simplicity"—'twas out of place;
> "Devotion" for an older face;
> Briefly, Selection smaller grew,
> "Vexatious! Odious!" none would do!
> Then, on a sudden, she espied
> One that she thought she had not tried:
> Becoming, rather—"edged with green"—
> Roses in yellow, Thorns between.
> "Quick! Bring me that!" 'Tis brought. "Complete,

Divine, Enchanting, Tasteful, Neat,"
In all the Tones. "And this you call——?"
"ILL-NATURE, Madame. It fits all."

AUSTIN DOBSON, *The Cap that Fits.*

A genuine growth of such diction would be of incalculable value to artists and public, in quickening and clarifying both interpretation and appreciation of verse. Many long comedy parts make less demand on the actor's skill. The listener, too, must be alert and sympathetic to follow such rapid pointing.

Coming a little nearer to lyric performance the most enormous variety of choice exists for the speaker —ranging from the mischief of Patrick Chalmers' "Old China" to the beautiful whimsicality of "The Stranger," so dear to the brotherhood of Izaak Walton, to De la Mare's "Peacock Pie," and all the lighter work of the Georgians.

When one recalls the sugary, sentimental doggerel, and the exaggerated and turgid tragedy, which dominated the penny reading of twenty years ago, there is much to be thankful for in this new movement towards grace and distinction.

The danger of such recitation is always realism. The story of the old Greek artist who painted his grapes so truly that birds flew in at the window to peck at them, but could not achieve the likeness of the boy who held them, so that it might frighten the thieves away, must stand as a warning for all dramatic speakers. If one character, one gesture, one pose, is "represented" instead of being suggested, the rest of the performance will lag behind into inanity.

Where two speakers combine, the delightful rhymed proverbs of Clifford Bax, with their inimitable chiming of far-fetched and whimsical rhyme, rank above any contemporary work. They are as apt as the dear old burlesque tags, as distinguished as Prior, as topical as "Max" himself.

They are a part of that delicate, wistful, gaiety which lit up the gloomy years with the "Poetasters of Ispahan" as the genius of Lovat Fraser lit up the dark London of the war, leaving us a memory of unforgettable charm.

An art of diction worthy to rank with these, would be the truest homage we could give to living writers and artists. For at its best such interpretation sets the living for a moment on a level with the greater dead, and if a genius be among them such opportunity may serve him, while he is yet alive to profit by recognition of his work.

So spoken, light verse is a veritable dance of words, and gives us the same sense of exhilarating and significant gaiety.

Among the technical forms instanced will be found the charming old French forms to which Henley and Gosse and Dowson gave a renewed vogue: the ballade, the splendid chant royal, the villanelle, the rondeau, with its variants, the rondel, and the tiny triolet, the sestina. These stand in the same relation to lyric poetry that Pierrot and Pierrette, Arlequin and Columbine stand to comedy. They are a convention so formal that it is always new. Each generation can interpret it afresh. Not a few arose out of the skeletons devised by the troubadours to help their improvisations. They gained new life in the North by their re-creation at the hands of Charles d'Orléans and François Villon, the "prince of all ballade-makers."

All owe their charm to three factors, interwoven rhymes, recurring rhythm, and the refrain.

The following short definitions will be of use to the student.

The Ballade. A poem consisting of three strophes, of eight
or of ten lines, followed by a verse of four or of
five lines, called the "envoy." A refrain at the end
of each strophe and of the envoy. In the perfect
ballade the refrain governs the length of the ballade.
A refrain of eight syllables implies eight lines in
each strophe. The same set of rhymes—arranged
ababbcbc—must recur in each strophe. No rhyme
word may recur. The envoy rhymes bcbc.

The sense of the refrain must be the keynote of
the whole ballade.

Here is an example of a modern ballade:

> Chicken-skin, delicate, white,
> .Painted by Carlo Vanloo,
> Loves in a riot of light,
> Roses and vaporous blue;
> Hark to the dainty *frou-frou*!
> Picture above, if you can,
> Eyes that could melt as the dew,—
> This was the Pompadour's fan!
>
> See how they rise at the sight,
> Thronging the *Œil de Bœuf* through,
> Courtiers as butterflies bright,
> Beauties that Fragonard drew,
> *Talon-rouge*, falbala, queue,
> Cardinal, Duke,—to a man,
> Eager to sigh or to sue,—
> This was the Pompadour's fan!
>
> Ah, but things more than polite
> Hung on this toy, *voyez-vous*!
> Matters of state and of might,
> Things that great ministers do;
> Things that, maybe, overthrew
> Those in whose brains they began;
> Here was the sign and the cue,—
> This was the Pompadour's fan!

ENVOY

Where are the secrets it knew?
Weavings of plot and of plan?
—But where is the Pompadour, too?
This was the Pompadour's *Fan*!
AUSTIN DOBSON, *On a Fan that belonged
to the Marquise de Pompadour.*

The ten-line ballade rhymes:

ababbccdcd ccdcd.

The strictest rules of the ballade have never been rigorously applied.

The chant royal is the greater form of ballade, with five verses of eleven lines and an envoy of five. As in the ballade, the envoy is an invocation to a prince or king.

The finest example in English is Edmund Gosse's magnificent *The Praise of Dionysus*. Here are the opening lines and the envoy:

Behold, above the mountains there is light,
A streak of gold, a line of gathering fire,
And the dim East hath suddenly grown bright
With pale aërial flame, that drives up higher
The lurid mists that, of the night aware,
Breasted the dark ravines and coverts bare;
Behold, behold! the granite gates unclose,
And down the vales a lyric people flows,
Who dance to music, and in dancing fling
Their frantic robes to every wind that blows,
And deathless praises to the vine-god sing.

ENVOY

Prince of the flute and ivy, all thy foes
Record the bounty that thy grace bestows,
But we, thy servants, to thy glory cling;
And with no frigid lips our songs compose,
And deathless praises to the vine-god sing.
EDMUND GOSSE, *The Praise of Dionysus.*

The villanelle is a poem of nineteen lines. Five three-lined stanzas and one of four, the refrain is taken from the first and third lines of the first stanza. The two alternately form the refrain of each verse from the second to the fifth, and both form the refrain of the quatrain.

The rondeau has thirteen lines of eight syllables only and two unrhymed refrains; three stanzas, consisting respectively of five, three, and five lines; the refrain after the second and third stanzas; rhymes:

aabba—aab and refrain—aabba and refrain.

The refrain must complete the thought of each stanza, and the line flows into it without a break. It is generally taken from the first half of the first line. This may serve as a model:

> Ma foi, c'est fait de moi, car Isabeau
> M'a conjuré de lui faire un rondeau.
> Cela me met en une peine extrême
> Quoi! treize vers, huit en *eau*, cinq en *ème*!
> Je lui ferais aussitôt un bateau.
>
> En voilà cinq pourtant en un monceau.
> Faisons-en huit en invoquant Brodeau,
> Et puis mettons, par quelque stratagème:
> Ma foi, c'est fait!
>
> Si je pouvais encor de mon cerveau
> Tirer cinq vers l'ouvrage serait beau;
> Mais cependant je suis dedans l'onzième:
> Et ci je crois que je fais le douzième;
> En voilà treize ajustés au niveau.
> Ma foi, c'est fait!
>
> VOITURE.

> You bid me try, BLUE-EYES, to write
> A Rondeau. What! forthwith? To-night?
> Reflect. Some skill I have, 'tis true;
> But thirteen lines!—and rhymed on two!—

"Refrain," as well. Ah, hapless plight!
Still there are five lines—ranged aright.
These Gallic bonds, I feared, would fright
    My easy Muse. They did, till you—
        You bid me try!

That makes them eight—The port's in sight:
'Tis all because your eyes are bright!
    Now just a pair to end in "oo,"—
    When maids command, what can't we do!
Behold! the RONDEAU—tasteful, light—
        You bid me try!

AUSTIN DOBSON.

Swinburne's "rondel" has eleven lines, Villon's twelve. Here are the rhyme variants:

aba refrain—bab—aba refrain. When the refrain is more than one line it rhymes with the b line:

abb—aab refrain—abba refrain.

The triolet consists of eight lines with two rhymes. One refrain occurs three times, here in the line order repeating line 1 three times:

1	2	3	1	4	5	1	2
a	b	a	a	b	b	a	b

In his arms thy silly lamb,
    Lo! he gathers to his breast!
See, thou sadly bleating dam,
See him lift thy silly lamb!
Hear it cry, "How blest I am!—
    Here is love and love is rest,"
In his arms thy silly lamb
    See him gather to his breast!

GEORGE MACDONALD.

I intended a hat,
And it turned to a bonnet,
In the shop as I sat
I intended a hat

My maid purchased *that*
With feathers stuck on it;
I intended a hat
And it turned to a bonnet.

A. STODART-WALKER, *Moxford Book of Verse.*

In all these forms it will be seen that the refrain is the most important and difficult to achieve: it must be spoken as an integral part of the thought and yet remain clearly a repetition. It is like the delight of watching a juggler play with balls. Each time it seems they must drop, and yet again they rise out of his hand.

But other refrains exist of a very different character. There is the "bourdon" or "drone," a low-pitched refrain hummed by the speaker under his breath to the bass of a musical accompaniment. Kingsley has an ineffective example in *Lorraine Lorrèe,*" generally omitted in modern editions.

Sometimes a "burden" consists of one or more words, as in the "Toll slowly" of *The Rhyme of the Duchess May* by Mrs. Browning, or Tennyson's "Oriana."

All such refrains must cut across the line with a monotonous music of their own. Only as the emotional stress of the form grows, the refrain swells with it, and fades, and dies, forming a musical echo to the sense. It must never be incorporated with the line, but must space and phrase the poem.

A third form is seen in the double refrain of *The Lady of Shalott.* There the refrain is part of the narrative and varies in significance and stress according to its meaning and place in the verse:

Listening, whispers, "'Tis the fairy
Lady of Shalott."

.   .   .   .

She saw the helmet and the plume,
  She look'd down to Camelot.

  .   .   .   .   .   .

And round about the prow she wrote,
  The Lady of Shalott.

  .   .   .   .   .   .

And her eyes were darken'd wholly,
  Turn'd to tower'd Camelot.
      Lord Tennyson, *The Lady of Shalott.*

This is not quite satisfactory; the refrain is a little intrusive and not musical enough in itself to decorate the lines. But it helps to mark strophic form and so it is popular, where a more formal structure would pass unnoticed.

In comedy the absurd intervention of the refrain adds to the charm of the metre. The compression required by some of the shorter poems, more especially the triolet, is favourable to perfect point and wit, and the form is irresistible when it is successfully achieved. Many freer variants give delightful stanzas.

Here is a very modern example where the stress varies most beautifully in each repetition:

I heard a bird at dawn
  Singing sweetly on a tree,
That the dew was on the lawn,
  And the wind was on the lea;
But I didn't listen to him,
  For he didn't sing to me.

I didn't listen to him,
  For he didn't sing to mè
That the dew was on the lawn
  And the wind was on the lea;
I was singing at the time
  Just as prettily as he.

> I was singing àll the time,
>   Just as prettily as he,
> About the dew upon the lawn
>   And the wind upon the lea;
> So I didn't listen to him
>   And he sàng upon a tree.
>
> JAMES STEPHENS, *The Rivals.*

Many gain their first introduction to poetry through satyric verse. It lacks the profoundest music of poetry, but it is a means of making the value of form clear to many who have never understood that verse is more than a convenient way of arranging words.

The faults of formal verse, its excessive reliance on sound, and its thin significance, become a positive advantage from this point of view. When the workmanship is good and the restraint of rule truly observed the result may be a very perfect thing.

One English work remains as the crown of all such poetry: FitzGerald's *Omar*, that blend of pathos and cynicism, of wit and philosophy, of irony and passion, which serves to lay bare a vanished civilisation to our sympathy and understanding. The form is perfect; always the three rising founts of rhyme, falling into pearls in the fourth line; always the twisted smile of half-ironical regret striking across the graver beauty of the ever-varying quatrain. Years of loving labour went to the perfecting of so beautiful a thing, and it stands as one of the glories of our more formal poetry, whether we reckon it as a translation, or as a reincarnation of its original. The last verse sums up in itself the whole genius of satyric poetry:

> And when Thyself with shining Foot shall pass,
> Among the guests star-scatter'd on the Grass,
> And in thy joyous Errand reach the Spot
> Where I made one—turn down an empty Glass!

CHAPTER X

THE SINGING OF ENGLISH WORDS

It was usual in the middle of the last century to regard English as an unmusical, inharmonious language, unsuited for the art of the singer. When an English song was to be given, the student was taught that a special pronunciation must be adopted; English could not be sung as it was spoken.

It would be interesting to examine the origin of so strange a belief. In part it may arise from the ghastly attempts at translation which were used on the operatic stage; here is a specimen from *Aïda*:

> Yet is there hope from this foul deed
> Thyself of disculpating.

There could indeed be little object in endeavouring to make these sentiments plain to any audience. The high standard of English dramatic and lyric verse made translations as a whole impossible, unless they could attain to something of the beauty of original verse. To reach such a standard without modifying the incidence of the musical pattern in the words was almost impossible. The majestic "Factum Est" of the *Messe des Morts*, for instance, reached in translation the pidgin-English form, "Done it is." Again, English does not lend itself readily to the divorce of sound and sense, so common in formal operatic and even oratorio singing, with its constant melodic repetitions and figure writing.

Where a single word was used to vocalise a long series of successive notes, or where an entire cadenza was sung on a single open vowel without regard to the original word from which it was derived, there was little encouragement to consider carefully the phonetic values of the language under execution.

Again, a succession of foreign influences dominated the minds of English musicians of standing for over two centuries. Handel, Italian opera, German *Lieder*, Wagner, the French *Chanson*, all these found their greatest interpreters among foreign-trained artists. In recitative, it is true, impeccable clearness was achieved, but at the sacrifice of pure melodic tone, and "declamation" was opposed to singing in technical training.

The foreign teachers, whose reputation as interpreters of their national music secured them the confidence of English pupils, the great foreign music-schools, all approached English as a foreign language, and their first endeavour was to bring it closer to their own standard of pronunciation. Rolled "r's," voiced final consonants, over-widened vowel shapes, lengthening of unstressed syllables, were among the devices which transmuted sung English into a kind of international Volapük. Nor was much help obtained from the stage diction of English players. Where it was not marked by the eccentricities of individual genius, it tended to a monotonous exaggeration which deprived it of any claim to be regarded, like that of the *Comédie française*, as the standard of national speech.

It was possible not many years ago to find an actor from that great institution supervising the speech training of deaf-mutes in order to ensure a high level of exactness in their French pronunciation. In England it would have been easier to find teachers of deaf-mutes superintending classes for the training of hearing students, under the delusion that the musical elements of speech are of no value in ordinary conversation. The pages of *Punch* give amusing evidence of the result: English people learnt to sing every language but their own. The great school of oratorio and festival singers at the end of the last century stood out as magnificent examples of rather formal diction, but it is, I believe, to the Gilbert and Sullivan operas, with their match- less blending of music and speech, that we owe the first perception that a singer could be audible and rapid, delicately accurate and simply expressive, in singing English, without sacrificing conviction or character, and without departing from the true phonetic values of his native tongue. The patter songs of *Patience* or the *Mikado* gave English singers the same kind of practice which had perfected the Italian *buffo* singer. The operatic singer might still assert that he was

Mahreed in Jahpahn,[1]

the ballad warbler might trill of "lawf," Mr. Corney Grain might convulse us with memories of the choir tenor whose voice was "so rich ! so syrupy !" that though he had been singing that one song for twenty years "no one had ever heard the words yet," but at the "Savoy" we could hear soloists, madrigal quartets, and chorus whose words were as audible and individual as speech.

Musical education brought a desire for the "setting" of better words. The study of Shakespeare in the theatre, and the historical study of music, brought a revival of appreciation for our great literature of English ballad music, which had never lost its hold on the popular taste. Opera companies formed a repertoire of translated opera. It was even interesting to be told, though one could not orally verify the fact, that *The Ring* was being sung in English at Covent

[1] Sir Hubert Parry on English singing.

Garden under the benediction of a great foreign con-
ductor who pronounced English the most singable of
modern tongues.

What foundation is there for the idea that the phonetic
values of one language are materially easier to sing than
those of another?

It seems to be rather the general character of
vocal utterance which prevails in any country, and
the extent to which the standard of ordinary speech
is accommodated to vocal utterance, that is in question.

There is reason to believe that the tremendous variation that exists in this respect has deep climatic and
racial causes; yet the working of the causes is not that
of the laws of nature. In all countries educated and
refined people perform the movements of speech with
greater accuracy and a stronger sense of rhythmic
values than uneducated people. Just as they perform
the movements of games, or of ordinary life, with a
greater natural ease and sense of style.

In all countries, free, untrammelled, primitive people
on the other hand perform the same movements with
a vigour and significance which the uneducated city-
dweller most of all lacks.

Prevalence of industrial conditions is bad for these
primitive artistic gifts, though, once the townsman is
trained, his quicker resourcefulness and sharper wits
make up for lack of early freedom.

Again, people of a warmer, less stern climate are
more prone to freedom of vocal utterance than those
enduring a cold or extreme temperature. The direct
effect of climate on the nature of breathing is very
marked; and the character of natural breathing has
an enormous effect on voice and so on speech.

Another contributing factor is the actual stage of
linguistic development at which a country stands. Is

its best speech the speech of scholars or of men of action?
Is the literary expression of the people as a whole
related to ordinary speech, as in the case of an early
civilisation, or to some artificial standard of a class
or court?

It is plain that all these considerations will have a
great effect in determining the degree of singableness
of a language as a whole, and especially its fitness as
a medium for song-writing.

But these are not the considerations generally present
the minds of those who say that English is unmusical.
They believe that the actual formation of English sounds
has an unfavourable effect on vocal tone.

The notes in Chapter V. will have already made it
clear that the fault lies not in the nature of English
vowel resonance as such, but in the fact that we accept
too slovenly a standard in the formation of our vowel
shapes, and that both socially and phonetically we are
inclined to accept certain clumsy movements, such as
a backward movement of the tongue in forming "aw"
and "ah," as inevitable in speech.

It must be repeated: speech in civilised communities
is in no sense a natural force obeying inevitable natural
laws, it is a thing taught by each generation to the
next; modification in utterance and standards have
been, and may be, achieved in the lifetime of a single
generation by deliberate early training.

The true function of the vowel sounds in any language
is to form a succession of musical resonances for the
voice; if this is done in ordinary speech, without exaggeration or violence, and with the principle of maintaining the best resonances that the form of the language
admits, it will be found that the difficulty of singing
English vowels disappears. The diagram in Appendix
II., inserted by kind permission of Dr. W. A. Aikin,

illustrates the formation of the vowel resonances in song. The large circle represents the full extent of the resonator: the distance between the palate and the lower jaw when the mouth is widely open as in the vowel "ah."

In the five first shapes the full extent of this resonator is modified by lip-rounding. First to the size of the little finger, then to the size of the thumb, and then to about the size of the first three fingers set closely together, one above the other two.

In the formation of "ah" the whole resonator is used. In the remaining shapes the resonator is modified by the arching of the tongue in successive levels. Throughout these changes the teeth should be kept apart at the same distance as in sounding "ah."

The directions already given in Chapter V. on the general character of the English vowels, will suffice to make the other elements of vowel-sound clear to the singer as to the speaker.

The positions of the English consonants, so far from being in themselves unfavourable to the voice, are distinctly easy. They are none of them markedly guttural; they can all be formed with a very lightly poised tongue; one at least, the characteristic "th," brings the tongue-tip more lightly forward and upward than in any Western European language. The English use of final "r," silent before a consonant, sounded before a vowel, helps to avoid glottal shock between two following words. The formation of initial "r" needs no uvular or guttural sound in English; the dialect coronal "r" of the West of England, on the other hand, is difficult to link with a pure vowel-sound, and the high trilled Scotch "r" clips the preceding vowel in speech and thins the tone in song.

The English nasal sounds are vocally excellent, "ng"

alone needing great precision if it is not to modify the preceding vowel too much.

There is unquestionably a tendency to get the general character of the voice a little white and breathy; this is corrected by the practice given in Appendix II. (page 250) for the formation of vowel sounds, and by constant practice of the forward nasal "m."

In all exercises for singing vowels, it is important to begin with the middle notes of the voice, and at first to keep within the compass of the speaking voice, constantly changing from song to speech, and from speech to song, constantly returning to the breathed vowel shapes, till the ear detects vowel quality and the true reinforcement of the voice by the vowel, finally trying for tone in the vowel.

It is above all important not to become "note-conscious" in regard to vowel sound. There is a tendency to feel "I can sing that note on that vowel" or "That vowel is easier on a high than on a low note." The vowel shaping must be like the fingering of the violinist's left hand; carried on independently of the right, though only through the dual action can the true note be formed. Almost all these difficulties in combination are due to involuntary contractions above the vocal chords, caused either by strained vocal production, or by an overflow of muscular energy in the formation of the vowels, at the moment of singing a loud or high note.

Take soft, medium notes first. Test and re-test the character of each movement till you are satisfied the change from song to speech does not necessitate a difference in the quality of the vowel-sound without your own intention. Then work for the special scale of your own voice, whatever its range may be, till you can balance every vowel perfectly at every pitch. A few special exercises of this kind will be found in Appendix II. (page 251).

Turning now to the verbal and syllabic structure of English, several difficulties do present themselves.

(1) The indeterminate character of final unaccented vowels.

(2) The undue prevalence of sibilants.

(3) The presence of double and triple consonant endings.

No. 1 is fully described in Chapter V.

With regard to No. 2, in addition to the six normal sibilant consonant groups, in English there is the custom of modifying "d" into "j" and "t" into "ch" before the vowel "u": "duke, duty, dew, dune, Tuesday, picture, tune," etc.—a tendency which it is still possible to resist. The modification of "t" into "sh" in attention, affection, etc., is a tendency too universal to be resisted.

Error in sibilant form is almost the most usual type of consonantal fault in English speech, and is, in many cases, due to faulty dentition. This introduces an element of weight and clumsiness into the diction of many singers, and in rough choral singing the protracted hissing is often suggestively vigorous.

These sibilants are present in nearly all plurals, in all possessives, and are constantly reiterated in triple consonant formation:

Rests, mists, frosts, hushed, guests, etc.

All these give triple consonants; a very heavy charge to certain syllables, as in the well-known hymn-line:

The breadth, length, depth and height to prove.

Some examples of special difficulty will be found in Appendix I. (page 252).

Passages thronged with such sounds are difficult to colour. The sounds "s" and "z" are the two sounds needing absolute closure of the nasal passages. They must therefore be very lightly touched and very carefully blended with the following vowel.

(4) The reduction of all vowel letters to a uniform sound in the case of the various spellings of the termination "er" (No. vii. əɪ), page 138.

"Father, altar, colour, satyr, dollar, nadir, incur," etc. This introduces a new vowel sound (in place of the combination "er"), intermediate between "u" in love and "a" in lack. But the "r" is clearly sounded in front of a following vowel. This is universal in educated English speech and must be maintained, even if we allow some variation in the degree of force to the "r" sound.

The group of completely elided endings in "en" has been dealt with in Chapter V. (page 129).

Notice the effect of singing

The sea, the sea, the òpen, òpen sea,

which should be the unstressed vowel slightly prolonged (No. vi. ə), and neither "opèn" nor "opùn." [1]

(5) The same vowel is heard in singing "castlĕ, whistlĕ, rustlĕ," where, as in "oftĕn" and "softĕn," the "t" is silent.

(6) The "e" in "wishĕs, goodnĕss, raisĕs, dancĕs, chasĕs, rosĕs, livĕst, strivĕst," require No. ix. (e), in singing, but must never be stressed. Agèd, kindrèd, raggèd, on the other hand, take a slight stress.[1]

(7) All the small connective words should be lightly monotoned in rhythm up and down the scale

[1] See page 133.

to get rid of the two opposed faults of indistinctness and overstressing:

Ex. "Ànd, to dò, fròm by wìth, as ìn, forasmùch às, of còurse, becaùse àlso, èven thùs, shàll wìll hàve, or dò."

If these and many other contracted variations are carried in singing to the point of actual elision, or to a point where the sound suggests a blur, the vocal effect is injured. But directly the attempt to give value to the vowel arrests attention, it is equally detestable. Generally such difficulties are due to bad setting, and here we come at last to the one real justification for the statement that English is difficult to sing.

It is particularly easy to sustain purely on English vowels for the whole value of the vocal note, touching off the following consonant at the end of the completed vocal tone, for the light detached quality of English consonants is very marked; what is not easy is to give to sung English the peculiarly synthetic character which we have already noted as the most marked characteristic of the spoken and literary speech of our day. English syllables are stressed with a degree of inequality which makes it almost impossible to restore them to clarity in singing. Not only is verbal unity dominant in English verse (*see* page 176), but all small unstressed words are robbed of their exact outline: as they fall in the course of any ordinary sentence of verse or prose, they have a value quite different from that of isolated words spoken without relation to their meaning. Example:

Oh the òak and the àsh and the bònnie ivy-trèe,
They floùrish at hòme in my aìn còuntriè.

The effect of attempting to restore that value for the sake of clarity in diction is most uncertain in effect.

At times it is quite good, at other times it suggests the
first steps of a child struggling with *Reading without
Tears*. When the musician, careless or ignorant of the
phonetic and logical values of the language, has confused quantity and accent and quality, broken verbal
unity and neglected stress - grouping, English suffers
more than any other language; for these things are
of the essence of our verse. We break up our speech
so little into syllables, that the effort to do so is at once
either comic, as in a patter song, or suggests a foreigner
singing our language.

In avoiding this mistake our drawing-room ballad-
singers, musical-hall artists, and light-opera singers,
constantly fall into the opposite error, of translating into
song the exact colloquial values of voiced consonants,
sustaining on liquids, vocalising "n" fully or curling
round the tongue on a final "r" or "l."

Here, then, is the work which has to be done by
composers, teachers and singers alike. To raise the
vocal values of spoken English on the one hand, to
respect the character of national speech on the other—
if the training of speech through the medium of vocal
tone were a part of every child's education, training
in spoken English preceding the specific teaching of
singing, recitation, or dramatic diction, this could very
simply be accomplished. Its effect on speech would
be not unlike the effect of universal good dancing-
teaching on movement.

Phonetic teaching in the mother-tongue is not always
sufficient. The work done by the phonetician is the
foundation of all scientific linguistic study and, above
all, of exact record. But applied to the mother-tongue
it may come too late, or be too much bound up with
the study of script; above all, it is still uneasy on the
question of any standard apart from common use, or

of any intrinsic goodness or badness in the character of speech - movement as a whole; with one or two brilliant exceptions, its professors neglect the element of vocal tone altogether.

For this the teachers of singing, of diction, and above all, of "elocution," have only themselves to blame. Preoccupied with our own fads and fancies, jealous of each other, afraid of open discussion or scientific investigation, we earned the contempt of the scientific inquirer from the first.

As a rule our so-called standards had no higher validity than personal taste, or a vague recollection of some popular performer's peculiarities. Spelling absurdities like "oft-ten," "soft-ten"; false derivations like "Eng-lish"; pedantries or absolute absurdities like "b-lü," or "mar-rage": all these lost for us the opportunity of being seriously consulted in the fundamental work of English phonetic. And when, in addition, ignorance of music earned for us the contempt of the musician, and the absence of the slightest element of literary taste made us an abomination to the scholar and the dramatist, we cannot wonder that the phonetician abandoned all effort to understand our methods, or accept our conclusions. Yet the true standard of a language lies in its capacity for vocal beauty. A standard which does not exclude or deprecate the existence, and the study and preservation of fine dialect forms, but aims at a national unity above and beyond these which should be worthy of our magnificent heritage of poetry and vocal music. That literature stands condemned which must seek for its medium archaic or pedantic forms, as so much of the literature of the mid-nineteenth century did. We want a vocal standard for the vulgar tongue, as well as a standard of vocabulary and construction. To speak as we sing, would soon make it easy to sing as we speak, and we should have once more, as in the sixteenth and seventeenth centuries, a school of English song-writers who understood their mother-tongue, and sought their inspiration in the work of her poets and not in the doggerel of her inferior versifiers.

The supposed conflict between vocal tone and diction is due to lack of sufficient mutual study and under-standing between singer, musician and speaker. The special qualities which should distinguish the singer are, in addition to his physical gifts and musical organ-isation, stability of intonation, purity of vowel quality, freedom in every muscular action required for the art of singing; precision and lightness in the attack and close of every movement; capacity for volume and intensity both in emotional appreciation and in ex-pressive tone. In a singer gifted by nature with a perfect organ, we are conscious of these things mainly as a sense of perfect balance. The quality of the low notes, for instance, is ringing as well as rich, the high notes are velvet-soft and full, not merely penetrating.

Words in relation to speech and song may be com-pared to the enlargement of a tiny photograph into a larger picture. Errors of detail which were imper-ceptible in the original snapshot show as disfiguring blurs in the large reproduction, yet both in reality are exactly correspondent.

The beauty of the finished picture depends on the clear definition of the original negative; if this was vague or inaccurate, not getting down to sufficiently fine detail, the increase in size, from lack of proportion, will show like a positive distortion, and no amount of retouching will give the real character of the original—only a conventional and wooden parody, having neither the merits of a photograph nor of a picture.

The more significant the subject, the more vividly the errors show; in a reproduction, for instance, of the human face, they would be at their worst and the enlargement becomes little less than a caricature.

So with the relation of song to speech, the vocal elements are stabilised in pitch, regulated in duration, measured in force, purified in quality, by prolongation and enlargement. The vowel elements must in like manner be stabilised in pitch, regulated in duration, measured in force and purified in quality, while the articulatory movements must attain a precision, but never an exaggeration, of position, force and timing.

It is useless to attempt to build an artificial accuracy of speech in song on a bad foundation of daily speech, because the result will lack the effect of true intention. The focus of attention will be shifted from the beauty of words and music to the thought, "I must speak well." Even long after the habit of good shaping, etc., has been established in song it will lack individuality because it will have no relation to the individual character and thought of the singer.

It is true that artistic expression presents a very curious phenomenon: the duplication of consciousness. Coquelin has summed it up admirably:

La *matière* de son art, ce qu'il travaille et pétrit pour en tirer sa création, c'est sa propre figure, c'est son corps, c'est sa vie. Il suit de là que le comédien doit être double. Il a son *un*, qui est l'instrumentiste; son *deux*, qui est l'instrument. Le *un* conçoit le personnage à créer, ou plutôt, car la conception appartient à l'auteur, il le *voit* tel que l'auteur l'a posé: c'est Tartuffe, c'est Hamlet, c'est Arnolphe, c'est Romeo: et ce modèle, le *deux* le réalise.

Ce dédoublement est la caractéristique du comédien.

Coquelin, *L'Art du Comédien*.

But there are limitations, and if the preoccupations of No. 1. are concentrated at too low a level of consciousness, imagination is hampered and a painstaking craftsman takes the place of the artist.

The singer must be a good everyday speaker. He must have "la parole de son chant"—the speech of his song. This is why so many singers lose all their charm when they are first trained to sing. They acquire an artificial imitation of their teachers' style instead of purifying their own natural diction.

Throughout these notes on speech the various good qualities have been shown to depend fundamentally on rhythmic control of movement, while again and again it has been necessary to reiterate that no external training can take the place of that inner mental emotional sensibility, which is the gift alike of thinker and of artist.

What becomes every day clearer is that the gift is more common by far than is supposed. A conclusion already plain to all who take the trouble to study the history of great periods of human achievement in art, in letters, or in religion.

To make our language-teaching the vehicle for such training, the medium for such expression, would in all certainty be one of the ways of combating the over-materialism of modern scientific education. The arts of song and of speech owe less homage than any arts to the need for material wealth, they touch the most human, and therefore the most divine, of our capabilities.

It has been the object of these notes to make the nature of our great gift of speech clearer and to show its relationship to all that makes life best worth living to the individual and to the nation.

APPENDIX I

THE poise needed for the practice of the following exercises is an easy erect position, balanced but not rigidly upright.

Correct the usual position from the feet up.

Lean slightly forward, looking down with head bent.

Shift the weight to the front, rather than the back, of the feet.

Draw the knees in, so that they are straightened rather than bent forward.

Slightly flex the body so that the hips are drawn back.

Gently raise the head, only drawing the chin very slightly in, and let the arms swing lightly in front of the hips.

Make no attempt to draw back the shoulders which will fall into their natural place, but work the head position carefully till it is perfectly easy to hold it erect.

I. Exercise for increasing the general flexibility of the chest before any special voice-breathing exercises are used.

In the good position, raise the hands lightly and rest the back of the first and second fingers against the chest, touching a point about two inches below the line of the breast bone. Close the thumbs gently against the first finger and leave the wrist quite relaxed. This is only to feel and not to influence the chest movement. Take and relax this position several times till it is natural and unstrained.

Breathe out, emptying the chest and relaxing as much as possible.

Breathe in, through the nose, evenly, at a normal rate of respiration and feel the sides of the chest swing out.

Breathe out; through the open mouth in the position

of " AH," relaxing and feeling a strong inward movement
of the chest wall. Breathe during the whole swing of the
chest, out and in, smoothly and without pause.

Repeat the double movement three times and rest,
repeat again three times and rest, repeat again three
times and rest. Then pass to another exercise.

II. Exercise for developing the general flexibility of
the abdominal muscles and improving the lines of
the chest.

Place the right hand flat on the top of the chest, the left
hand flat about three inches below the waist. Without
breathing in or out consciously, draw in and then relax
the muscles under the lower hand. The upper hand will
then be pressed very slightly forward. Repeat this exercise,
counting "òne, two; òne, two," etc., stressing the inward
contraction of the muscles. The hands must just feel, but
never assist, the movement of the muscles in any way.

III. Exercise for strengthening the palate muscles.

Sound clearly the two syllables

" AH " (ɑː) and " NG " (ŋ). *Repeat* 20 *times.*
Keep the tip of the tongue closely against the lower front
teeth, and avoid widening or contracting the lips.

Repeat the syllables in a clear whisper. *Repeat* 20 *times.*

Breathe in at "NG" and out at " AH," 20 *times;* still
keeping the tongue-tip carefully in position, and avoiding
any undue breath friction. Listen for a light click between
the first and second syllables in the last series. This sound
is a click of the palate, not of the vocal membranes, and
must not be as strong as " K."

IV. First exercise for sustaining. After both breathing
exercises have become quite easy.

Position as for I.; hands as in II.

Breathe in as in I., keeping the right hand on the side
of the chest. Shift hand to top of the chest, and breathe
out slowly with a soft full sound of " AH "; gently press
back the abdominal muscles, and leave the ribs as fully

expanded at the end of the expiration as at the beginning. Sustain for five seconds.

Be careful to study the description of the correct movements of expiration in Chapter V. very exactly before doing this exercise. The abdominal muscles must never be allowed to retract during inspiration, or to bulge forward below the waist. The muscles retract during expiration, gently pressing back the diaphragm to its place, the ribs remaining expanded till the exercise is finished and then relaxing in their turn.

There is a distinct forward movement between the ends of the lowest ribs above the waist during inspiration (epigastric movement).

V. Exercise for attack of the note.

Free inspiration as at I.

Hum the sound of " M " very softly on middle " A "; the expiratory movement must be performed entirely by the abdominal muscular force, pressing the diaphragm gently upward, and not by the relaxing of the rib muscles pressing in the sides of the chest.

The throat is not felt to take any part in this exercise. The lips remain at rest, the tongue-tip rests lightly against the lower front teeth. The teeth are slightly parted behind the lips.

Directly the exercise is mastered rest the finger against the lips, and feel a constantly increasing vibration within the lips. The air passes softly out through the nose. The sound of the note must begin on the very instant of the expiratory movement. No scrape or puff of air must precede it. The former gives "shock," the latter breathy, tone.

VI. Repeat the exercise down the scale for six notes, in the key of C, ending on middle C.

VII. Conclude practice with the full scale, octave C to C, up and down, on " M."

VIII. Sentence exercise on sustaining.

The following example taken from Collins' *Ode to the Passions* forms a good exercise in sustaining. Speak in one breath:

   i. Pale Melancholy sat retired.

   ii. Pale Melancholy sat retired, and in notes by distance made more sweet.

   iii. Pale Melancholy sat retired, and in notes by distance made more sweet poured through the mellow horn.

   iv. Pale Melancholy sat retired,
       And . . .
     In notes by distance made more sweet
       Poured through the mellow horn her pensive soul.

This last sustained breath should last for twelve seconds.

IX. Exercise in heavy syllabic charge.[1]

Articulate clearly the following words:

Copts, fifths, acts, chaise, sixths, sevenths, tenths, thousandths, lengths, guests, hosts, posts, sects, exist'st, striv'st.

See also the syllables and sentences suitable for children in Appendix II.

X. Practise carefully the word-lists in the chart on pp. 138–9 and the illustrative examples in Chapter V.

[1] These lists and several other exercises are printed in a leaflet for class use (*First Notes on Speech Training*), and have been reproduced by permission of Messrs. George Allen and Unwin.

APPENDIX II

EXERCISES IN PROSODY

1. Mark the stresses of the first nine and a half lines of *Paradise Lost*.

2. Complete the scansion in stress-feet of the hymn quoted on page 176.

3. Find twenty examples of short unaccented syllables followed by long accented syllables.

Twenty of short accented syllables followed by long unaccented, etc.

4. Mark the long unstressed syllables in the first verse of Ariel's song, " Come unto these yellow sands " (*The Tempest*, Act I. Scene ii).

5. Write in musical notation the lines:

" Methought the billows spoke and told me of it," etc.
                    The Tempest, Act III. Scene iii.

Rewrite the notation in exact musical time, and speak the lines to it. See Chapter VII., pp. 170–177.

6. Mark the stresses and write in musical notation this line from Shelley's poem, *The Question*:

" But kissed it and then fled, as thou mightest in dream."

7. Contrast the musical notation of each of the eleven forms of verse in the *Midsummer Night's Dream* in Chapter VIII.

The Resonator Scale

The diagram on p. 249 illustrates the formation of the fundamental vowel resonances.

The first four shapes are made by lip-rounding. The next (AH) is neutral; the mouth being opened to about the width of two fingers, the tongue-tip lying lightly against the lower front teeth, above the gum, the lips not in any way shaped or drawn back.

In vi., vii., and viii., the tongue-tip remains in

the same position, the middle of the tongue arching gently up. In the last four the tongue-tip remains in position, but the sides of the tongue touch the upper side teeth, the middle of the tongue arching more and more toward the roof of the mouth.

If the six vowels

I.	II.	III.	V.	X.	XII.
OO	OH	AW	AH	EH	EE

are whispered clearly, the teeth being kept apart as at AH, while the movements of lip-rounding and tongue-arching are carried out as directed, the sounds of the vowels will be heard to produce a definite scale of pitch variation, the fundamental pitch resonances of these vowels.

OO. I.   OH. II.   AW. III.   AH. V.   EH. X.   EE. XII.

All the vowels of the scale can be heard in musical succession in the same manner.[1]

Any modification in the position of the organs of articulation results in an immediate modification of the pitch vibration, and so of the position of the vowel in the resonator scale.

The efforts of the student are directed to producing each resonance at its most central point.

Students who have become accustomed to their own defective quality of vowel sound, and can no longer detect it clearly, will readily recognise the error in pitch when whispering. Correcting it, they very readily pass from a whispered to a sung note, and so recover the correct fundamental position of the vowel sound.

[1] See *The Voice, an Introduction to Practical Phonology*. Dr. W. A. Aikin. Longmans, Green & Co.

DIAGRAM OF THE RESONATOR SCALE

by permission of Dr W.A. AIKIN.

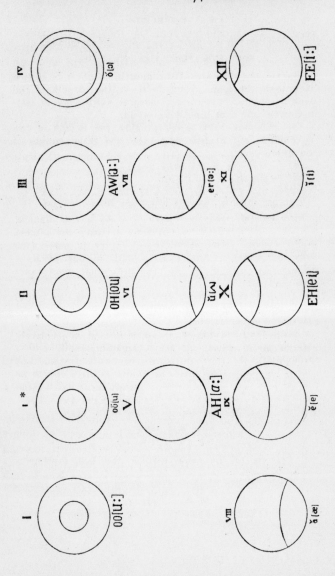

Exercises

1. Breathe the six main vowel sounds as follows:

Hoo, Hoh, Haw, Hah, Hay, Hee.

Observe the rules that the tongue must never be drawn back from the lower front teeth, or the corners of the mouth retracted beyond their natural width when at rest, in English vowel or diphthong sound.

The following table gives roughly the extent of the lip-rounding to be observed in the first three vowels of this group:

OO to the size of the little finger.

OH to the size of the thumb.

AW to the size of the first and third fingers drawn together, with the second finger placed above them.

After forming the vowels very carefully in this manner, breathing as indicated in Appendix I., play the pitches of the vowels, listen attentively, and try to make each whispered vowel conform exactly to its musical pitch. A tuning-fork will make this exercise much more exact than any piano.

2. Repeat this exercise, gently diminishing the initial " H " and making a soft smooth attack as in the " M " practice in Appendix I.

Continue till the shapes can all be formed consecutively without jar or effort, the teeth remaining easily parted throughout.

It is very important that the mouth position should be easy at first, and not too widely opened till it has become quite natural not to close the teeth on " EE " and " EH."

3. Alternate the extreme positions of the scale:

OO—AH—OO
EE—AH—EE, etc.

4. Practise in the same manner the four diphthong combinations.

I	OW	OI	U
vi. xi	v* i*	III. xi	xi. I
Time	Town	Toil	Tune

5. Add all the subordinate vowels in their proper order.

6. Study attentively the character of the breath resonance; watch the tongue position to avoid throaty sound. Watch the lip position and the free passage of the air through the mouth to avoid nasal sound. See also exercises for breathing, Appendix I.

7. Sing each vowel on a descending scale of six notes, from middle A to middle C, in the key of C. See Ex. V. p. 245.

Begin with OO, OH, AW, AH, EH, EE, in this order. Then take the diphthongs, sustaining on the first half of the first three, and on the second half of the fourth.

Note that the initial sound of this combination is little more in speech than a " Y " glide.

8. Add at the end of each descending scale a lightly vocalised ascending scale, to the octave C and down again.

9. Change very gently on the return to middle C, from song to speech, retaining the musical pitch.

10. Repeat this exercise, substituting a monosyllabic spoken word for the sung vowel. Repeat till the quality of the word is as pure as that of the sung vowel.

11. Monotone lightly a sentence, or two lines of verse, having the same vowel as its predominant sound.

12. Speak freely a passage of verse in which the selected vowel strongly predominates.

Example for " OO "—Tennyson's *Lady of Shalott*:

" She left the web," etc.

For " AW ": Lines from the *Jackdaw of Rheims*.

The vowels " Eh," " Oh," " ĕ "; the diphthongs " Ow," and " I," will be found specially susceptible to nasal tone.

The vowels " Aw," " Ah," " ŏ "; and the diphthong " Oi," will be found specially susceptible to throaty sound.

The vowels " Ah " and " ă " are those in which shock of the glottis most often occurs, particularly when they stand as initials.

The vowel " OO " is the sound in which it is easiest to detect breathy quality.

The whole vowel scale and not only selected sounds must be worked, to overcome these and other mistakes.

Northern speakers tend to make the following transpositions: " bid " into " bed "; " bed " into " bad "; " bad " into the initial sound of the diphthong " I," intermediate between " ŭ " and " Ah " (phonetic clear a).

Southern speakers tend to make the following transpositions: " bad " into " bed "; " bed " into " bid "; " bid " into a narrow " beed."

Cockney sounds vary between excessive nasalisation —a fault common to many town accents—and the complete absence of any nasal resonance.

Exaggeratedly refined voices are prone to a throaty sound, the result of a tongue too rigidly depressed, and a constricted throat.

The sentence, " Mr. Shaw saw a tall form fall on the shore," is a good test for this particular difficulty.

The following exercises will be found useful for training children:

1. Vowels and Consonants.

Oot	oht	awt	aht	ayt	eet
Ood	ohd	awd	ahd	ayd	eed
Oop	ohp	awp	ahp	ayp	eep
Oob	ohb	awb	ahb	ayb	eeb
Oof	ohf	awf	ahf	ayf	eef
Oov	ohv	awv	ahv	ayv	eev
Ook	ohk	awk	ahk	ayk	eek
Oog	ohg	awg	ahg	ayg	eeg

("g" is hard.)

Oos	ohs	aws	ahs	ays	ees
Ooz	ohz	awz	ahz	ayz	eez
Oosh	ohsh	awsh	ahsh	aysh	eesh
Ooge	ohge	awge	ahge	ayge	eege

("ge" *as in* "rouge.")

Ooch	ohch	awch	ahch	aych	eech

("ch" *as in* "each.")

Ooj	ohj	awj	ahj	ayj	eej

("j" *as in* "judge.")

Oost	ohst	awst	ahst	ayst	eest
Oosts	ohsts	awsts	ahsts	aysts	eests
Ooth	ohth	awth	ahth	ayth	eeth
Ooths	ohths	awths	ahths	ayths	eeths
Oodth	ohdth	awdth	ahdth	aydth	eedth
Oodths	ohdths	awdths	ahdths	aydths	eedths
Oom	ohm	awm	ahm	aym	eem
Oon	ohn	awn	ahn	ayn	een

Strike the left hand lightly on the palm of the right, keeping the latter quite still but not rigid. Articulate the vowels as the sound of the clapping is heard and the consonants as the left hand swings away again to the left with a free relaxed movement. Keep exact time.

Cut a small wedge of cardboard about three-quarters of an inch wide and tapering to a point. Hold the wide end lightly between the finger and thumb, and pass it between the teeth at the instant when the vowels in the following syllables are articulated, except in the case of "she"; here swing the hand away from the body in exact time with the previous movement.

2. Wedge.

Sa	ka	she	fa	ra
Ka	ka	she	fa	ra
Ra	ka	she	fa	ra
Da	ka	she	fa	ra
Pa	ka	she	fa	ra
Fa	ka	she	fa	ra

The following sentences provide amusing practice for children:

SENTENCES FOR DAILY PRACTICE

1. The poor dog's paw poured water from every pore.
2. The liar says he can play the lyre.
3. The Duke paid the money due to the Jew before the dew was off the grass on Tuesday, and the Jew having duly acknowledged it said adieu to the Duke for ever.

4. A dire misfortune befell the dyer.

5. There is a layer of bones in the lion's lair.

6. Is that the Lord Mayor's mare? The mower goes more on the moor.

7. She is a thistle sifter, and she has a sieve of sifted thistles, and a sieve of unsifted thistles, because she is a thistle sifter.

8. She sells sea-shells, sherry, and sand-shoes.

9. She sees a shot-silk sash-shop, full of Surah silk sashes, where the sun shines on the shop signs.

10. Should such a shapely sash such shabby stitches show?

11. The suitability of a suet pudding without superfluous plums is a superstition presumably due to Susan's true economy.

12. This lute, with its flute-like tones, was captured in the loot of a great city, and its luminous sides are made of unpolluted silver.

13. Laid in the cold ground all night it lay an ice-drop there.

14. Last year I could not hear with either ear.

15. His beard descending swept his aged breast.

16. He is literally literary.

17. Which witch had the wen on her hand when we met them, and you asked them whether we should have fine weather?

18. She says she shall sew a sheet.

19. I snuff shop snuff, do you snuff shop snuff?

20. Was that your ewer of yore?

21. He generally reads regularly in a government library particularly rich in Coptic manuscripts except during the month of February.

These sentences and exercises, originally devised by the author, have been printed by Miss Wellesley-Reade in her excellent "Word Practice" books; they are reproduced here by her kind permission.

PRINTED BY THE TEMPLE PRESS AT LETCHWORTH IN GREAT BRITAIN